WHAT'S LEFT
OF DON

WHAT'S LEFT OF DON

A MEMOIR

DONALD J. HURZELER

Kua Bay Publishing LLC

First Edition

Print ISBN 978-0-9981063-6-6

eBook ISBN 978-0-9981063-7-3

DEDICATION

I dedicate this book to those who have accepted me for who and what I am for all these decades...my friends. You know who you are and, just in case I have never mentioned it, I love you. And if you wonder if I meant to include you in the "friends" category, I did.

I want also to dedicate this book to all my teammates over the years... schoolmates, athletes, teachers, coaches, mentors, bosses, peers, employees, volunteers...all of you. You made me who I am today, for better or worse, and I value each and every one of you.

I am grateful for each person in my life, past and present. Collectively, you make up my life experience. Thank you.

TABLE OF CONTENTS

CHAPTER ONE

What's Left of Don...
An Explainer About What This Book is About

I am a guy who has wandered through the lives of a lot of people. Perhaps you are one of those who shared time and space with me. More likely, you wouldn't know me from a hole in the ground. Either way, we have things to discuss.

My life will make you laugh, cause you to shake your head, make you wonder if I am writing about your life and probably encourage you to no end. If I can keep a smile on my face for all these decades, heck...anyone can. So, I am going to offer up my life to you, in bite-sized pieces, for you to enjoy, spit out or just chew on.

What I am about to offer is the absolute truth, but it is the truth as I see it. That may often differ slightly/hugely from the actual truth. Unfortunately, I learned early on that a good story can only get better with the addition of details, both real and manufactured. I'll do my best to stick to the real truth whenever I can recall it. Actually, I neither know, nor give a damn, about true accuracy. I'm here to tell stories the way I remember them, and that is the truth to me.

I sometimes think of myself as the person who was 17th from the top of the command for building the Great Pyramid of Giza. I did participate in important and big things...like running billion-dollar businesses. However, although I certainly started at the very bottom, I never got to visit the very top. I always thought of my spot as close enough to the top to influence those there, help them formulate and achieve their vision, and enjoy some of the benefits of being that high up the chain. BUT I always knew full well that my 17th place in the chain could easily be filled by that person in 18th place and, after a few weeks, it would be like I had never been there. There would be only one carrier of the Story of Don

1

as history rolled along, and that would be me. So...before I head out for that final exit interview in life, hopefully a few decades yet down the road, here are bits and pieces of my story. Together, they add up to What's Left of Don.

CHAPTER TWO

Shit Happens at the Sears Store

Everyone tells me that I was a cute little kid. I was tall for my age, at age two. I had beautiful red hair with a wave in the front. Folks still tell me how friendly I was and how smart for a little shaver. I guess these were the reasons that the Sears incident was such a shock to all involved.

It was fall in L.A. I was asked to accompany my parents on a shopping trip. This was not an ordinary shopping trip. On this very special day, we would go to Sears.

The Inglewood, California, Sears store was a heartstopper. It was as fancy as thing got in 1950. They even had a guy in a little booth up on the roof who would direct you to an open parking space ("Please turn right then left at the first aisle."). Parking aisles...I always liked that term.

Outside the store was "AUTOMOTIVE." As a two-year-old, I could only guess at what complex procedures took place in that facility. But inside the Sears store was where the real action happened.

Popcorn was the name of the game. You could smell it the moment you entered the door. Fresh, hot popcorn. First order of business, get that popcorn.

Next, trail that popcorn throughout the store. This may have been done on purpose, so people could find their way back to the exit. These were big stores and you could get lost. No matter, the popcorn on the floor was always closer to my hand than the popcorn in my dad's hand. That trail of other people's popcorn made the whole shopping experience feel like a treasure hunt.

I remember thinking that I should not have eaten all those dates with my high-fiber cereal so soon before leaving on the shopping trip. I remember feeling alone and in need of a bathroom while my parents negotiated with the refrigerator salesman. I can also recall my true amazement that any store would have rows of free-standing toilets right out in the middle of the sales floor. How convenient.

People say that I used to hum while going to the bathroom. It bothers me that they would know that little fact. I do not even know some of these people.

Let's say that the hum recollectors were correct. There I sat, in the middle of a busy sales floor, short pants down around my little Buster Browns, humming to myself and off-loading a couple of bowls of Shredded Wheat and dates.

My folks remember that it was a fairly remarkable output for such a small child. My theory is that some other kid or, dare I theorize, some lazy salesman, had already dropped a load in the Kenmore commode. Either way, I do remember that the lack of toilet paper presented one of my first problem-solving opportunities.

Now, up to this point in my life, my parents had been pretty affirming, in fact downright congratulatory of my bathroom successes. This little incident put a stop to that good practice. To this day, I've not received another pat on the back for a poop well done. Heck of a shame, really.

When I think of Sears, I think of the guy up on the roof directing traffic, of the smell of popcorn and its free availability to anyone enterprising enough to just pick it up off of the floor, and of that gleaming white toilet. I also think about the formerly nice salesman in the short-sleeved white shirt and black tie, toupee slightly askew, looking into the toilet and having what I learned later on was a shit fit.

We never returned to the Inglewood Sears store.

And is there a lesson to be learned by my early mistake? Yup, Sears should never have gotten rid of the prominently placed popcorn machine. You know what those stores smell like now? Neither do I.

CHAPTER THREE

Meeting My First Celebrity

If you were born and raised in Los Angeles, California, in the 1950s and 1960s, you could not avoid meeting celebrities. They lived in your neighborhood, went to your stores and did everything they could to actually be seen. We had a huge black-and-white TV. I watched it hours each day. Even when I was a kid, there were celebrities that I absolutely loved and I did everything I could to meet them.

For reasons I never completely figured out, my parents pretty much gave me the run of the neighborhood. By that I mean they really didn't keep track of me. I walked several blocks to school, by myself, in kindergarten. Freely walked to the market whenever I could get my sweaty little hands on a nickel for candy. Visited friends' homes blocks away. I was a handful at home and I suspect they were just happy to have me out of their hair for hours at a time.

So, with my love of the rich and famous, and my complete freedom to wander around, I sought out my first celebrity. Mom had mentioned that Bill Welsh was bringing his show, *Star Shoppers,* to a supermarket just a few blocks from our house in Inglewood, California. That was all I needed. The next day, I was there, age five or so and all by myself, an hour before the show started. And what a show it would be. Mr. Welsh played all kinds of silly games with the audience (about 100 percent women in those days) and they could win full bags of groceries. More about those full bags later.

But the hell with Mr. Welsh...nobody told me that the one and only Little Oscar would be there WITH his fabulous Wienermobile. In fact, he was already there. And there, before my unbelieving eyes, was THE Wienermobile. The door on the side of the wiener was open. Could Little Oscar be inside? Time to find out.

I ran as fast as my little legs would take me to the Wienermobile. No one around it, but I could hear voices inside. I yelled up, "Is Little Oscar in there?" "Come on in" was the reply. I walked into the Wienermobile, adjusted my eyes to the change in light and looked in the direction of the voice. I almost passed out—there was Little Oscar! He was propped up in the passenger seat and he was smoking a big cigar. Another guy stood near the driver's seat...probably the driver. However, my focus was 100 percent on the man himself...Little Oscar. He greeted me, shook my hand and asked me if I was there for the show. I'm not sure if I even said a word. I just smiled and could not believe my luck. And then two things happened that surprised and delighted me. First, he reached in his pocket, found a Wiener Whistle and gave it to me. My own Weiner Whistle. Life can get no better. Next, he thanked me for coming (in other words...see you later, kid) and I turned to go. But Little Oscar had one more big surprise for me before I left, a surprise for him as well. As he attempted to stand up to show me the door, he let loose with one of the loudest farts I have ever heard. There were about three seconds of silence as we looked at one another, and then the three of us burst into the longest, loudest laughter that I can ever remember. I would like to tell you that it smelled like a Smokie Link, but my memory doesn't provide that much detail. All I remember was this great big celebrity (they don't get any bigger than Little Oscar when you are a five-year-old kid) farted just like the rest of us and then had the good sense to enjoy the moment.

The Star Shoppers show was fun and exciting. I got to see how they did a live remote. I got to see Mr. Welsh read his commercials off the shopping bags they used for cue cards. Mr. Welsh signed and gave me one of those shopping bags. And I learned a little secret about the show....

The big prizes for the show were shopping bags brimming with groceries. And here is the little secret...I got to watch them fill those great big shopping bags. They started on the bottom with three rolls of paper towels, placed horizontally in the bag. That served two purposes—it made the bags easy to hold and it almost completely filled them up. A few dazzling items (Oscar Mayer All Beef Wieners, a carton of Lucky Strike cigarettes and a loaf of Wonder Bread) stuck out of the top of the bag. I'm guessing the total value of the whole prize was less than $5 in 1952 money. And, the cancer was thrown in for free.

I learned a lot that day. Since then I have met or been around more famous and infamous people than just about anyone I know...presidents, Nobel Prize winners, stars, local, national and world-wide celebrities. None impressed me more than Little Oscar. Of course, none of them farted in my presence...that could have made the difference.

CHAPTER FOUR

The Beginning of My Writing Career

Even as a kid, I loved people who could write succinctly and with humor. I loved an old columnist named Walter Winchell. He wrote short, right-to-the-point sentences about the latest gossip or happenings of the day. He put enough of them together each day to produce the number one newspaper column of his time.

In Los Angeles in the 1960s, we had two newspapers...the *L.A. Times* and the *Los Angeles Herald Examiner*. The *Herald* got delivered in the afternoon and tended to be a bit more tabloid than the proper morning paper, the *Times*. I loved them both.

The *Times* had a columnist who wrote a bit like Walter Winchell, but nonetheless he did have his own distinct style. His name was Matt Weinstock and I read his column every day. When the time was right, I started sending him short little items that he might want to include in his column. Sent them typed up and by snail mail...no email in those days. If I was lucky, several days later I would pick up the *Times* and read one of my stupid little items in his column. I recall one of them read: "Don Hurzeler of Palos Verdes Estates wrote to say that if inflation gets any worse, it might be cheaper just to eat the money."

Well, turns out I liked seeing my name in one of the top newspaper columns on the West Coast. I sent him more and more. Some he would skip because they were probably just plain stupid or horrible, but others he ran, much like the lame one above. Several months into this long-distance relationship, he called me and told me how much he appreciated my items. Told me he felt guilty not being able to pay me for them. Asked if I could join him for lunch at the Brown Derby restaurant. Back in the day, the Brown Derby was THE place all the stars went to be seen. I immediately accepted and asked if he would mind if I brought my mom along. There was quite a long silence. "Why would you bring your mom along?" was his reply. I said, "Because she is my ride." Another lengthy silence. "Why would you need her to drive?" he asked. "Because I am 12 and don't yet have my license."

This turned out to be the first time I ever heard the expression "Are you shitting me?" "Well, no, I am not shitting you. I will be thirteen in a few weeks, but will still need a ride." The conversation went straight downhill after that.

Mr. Weinstock explained to me that he would be the laughing stock of the newspaper business WORLDWIDE if it were ever revealed that he was getting his content from a twelve-year-old kid. I could tell this wasn't up for debate. He seemed on the verge of panic. Needless to say...no Brown Derby for Donny. No more inclusion in the nifty column written (for the most part) by Matt Weinstock In fact, I noticed that he almost never ran anything from anyone other than himself after our little episode.

Mr. Weinstock filed his last column many years ago and passed away. I feel that he would not object to my sharing this with you now, given that he expired in 1970. I kept it to myself for more than 50 years and it is not really a matter of national security. So there it is...Little Donny and Matt Weinstock and our almost-luncheon at the Brown Derby.

CHAPTER FIVE

An Uncareful Life

"Careful" would not describe me. I was born with WAY too much energy. I am wired to do things fast, leaving behind the things that slow me down, like research and preparation. Now this will come as a shock, but all of that has often resulted in personal injury, accidents where I am the one, the only one, limping away from the scene. I've had more stitches than a quilt. Broken most of the body parts a human can break. Emergency rooms love me.

Hard to put a good spin on this, but the truth is that I am less than careful on purpose. I've seen a lot of people spend their whole lives operating in the safety zone. Too me, that is not a whole life, it is part of a life. I want to see it all. And in my case, getting to see it all usually involves bandages at some point.

Knowing I survived all of the accidents I am about to describe, feel free to enjoy them. Heck...some are so stupid they even make me laugh. Like...

A man and an axe...what could possibly go wrong?

The first house my wife and I bought had a fireplace. We had no money for wood, so I decided to drive into the forest to chop my own firewood. I'm not real sure I had ever been in a forest prior to this adventure, and I know for sure I had never chopped wood. First stop, the hardware store to buy an axe. Next stop, the forest, some fifty miles away.

We drove up into the mountains and found a likely spot. I asked my wife to stay with the car and keep watch for us—I was not exactly sure of the legality of my wood-taking. She was to honk if potential trouble approached, say, a cop or a forest ranger. Me, I went down the side of the hill, well out of sight of the car, found an already downed tree and began to swing away at one of the branches.

Who knew that a loose limb might snap up into the air when I hit it as hard as I could with that axe? Not me. A big piece of wood broke off, flew up, hit me in the forehead and knocked me out cold. From the amount of blood on my face and upper torso when I finally woke up, this scene must have looked like an assassination attempt. Enough blood that I had to wipe it out of my eyes to even see where I was. Turns out I was resting on a downed tree limb with an axe lying nearby. I wasn't real sure what I was doing there.

I crawled up the hill to our car. My wife was horrified when she saw me. She told me I had been down there so long that she suspected I had chopped more wood than we could transport. I told her that would not be a problem and could she please drive us to the nearest hospital. She inquired as to the whereabouts of my brand new axe. I assured her we would never ever need that axe again and please start driving before I bleed out.

That is the kind of "uncareful" I am known for.

There is more...

Nude beach debacle

I was going surfing when I took the wrong trail down the steep cliff to Black's Beach in La Jolla, California. Back then, Black's was also the world's biggest nude beach. I can assure you that had nothing to do with my decision to surf there. But back to the wrong trail—that wrong trail turned into a narrow half a trail that went almost straight down the side of the cliff. No way I could hold onto my surfboard (lots of wind rushing up that cliff) and stay on that trail. Unfortunately, the trail was hard-packed and covered in loose sand, slippery as could be. I had on my low-grip bare feet...probably should have worn some shoes. I started slipping and sliding and quickly realized that I had a choice—let go of my board and slide all the way to the bottom of the trail or go flying off the 800-foot cliff, which I assumed might result in some significant injuries. I let go of the board, forgetting that it was attached to me by a leash, squatted down, and surfed my two bare feet all the way to the bottom.

My quick trip down the hill dragging along a once beautiful and somewhat expensive surfboard did not go well. When I hit the beach, the surfboard looked like it had gone through a cheese grater. It was missing a fin and lots of fiberglass and had dings all over it. My bare feet looked much the same. There was not a single piece of callus or skin left on the bottom of either foot. They were a bloody mess.

It turns out that nude people on a beach are not all that interested in helping some idiot with a beat-up surfboard and two hamburgers for feet. In those days, there was no lifeguard on duty to help me out. All I had was an increasingly large crowd of naked people, mostly male, mostly way overweight. Most of them looked like I had seen them on America's Most Wanted. They did point out the safer trail and suggested I could crawl up to the top of the cliff dragging the board along behind me. There was some laughter around the fact that "dragging couldn't really hurt that board."

I did manage to drag the board and myself up that 800-foot cliff. Crawled over to my car and drove all the way back to Orange County using my raw feet to work the brakes, gas and clutch. It took weeks for the feet to heal and about half a paycheck to fix the board. That was my last trip to Black's Beach.

Asshole meets sharp metal object...a moment to remember

Ever put a sharp-ended steel file into a rubber ball for no apparent reason, leave it on the couch and forget you put it there? I did. I found it, too. Jumped on the couch. The file absolutely hit the bullseye in my butt and I jumped straight up in the air. I think I was about four at the time. I'm sure my grandmother still has nightmares about having to clean that wound, and she has been dead about thirty years. A steel file poked directly into your asshole will get your full attention.

I would tell you more, but I promise you don't really want to know more than I have already told you. Let's move on.

Using a commercial-grade high-pressure air hose to clean a wound... whoops!

I'm guessing you have never used a high-pressure industrial-strength air hose to clean debris out of a wound. I did. I was working a summer job in a metal shop, wearing work overalls with a pocket chest high in the front. There was a sharp lead pencil in that pocket. As I reached across my chest for something, I stabbed my forearm with the sharp pencil, and the lead broke off under the skin. I could see it there and I thought that lead in my flesh might not be too good for me. So, I picked up an air hose and pointed it into the hole where the pencil lead was now residing. The giant blast of air separated the skin from my arm and blew my entire forearm up into a huge bubble. Took less than a second. I looked like Popeye. There is no way to exaggerate how odd this looked...like I had a balloon just under the skin of my forearm.

I had been told to never use that air hose for anything on my body, not even just to blow off metal shavings. I was told that I would be fired for the first such offense. I considered that possibility for about five seconds before walking over to my boss to show him my predicament. He grabbed his pocket knife and poked the skin pretty hard. Out leaked some of the air. Now I had an air bubble that I could squeeze and make move up and down my arm. Pretty darn cool. There was some worry about my getting air into my blood stream (apparently that kills you), so off I went to the hospital.

I was their first-ever case of "air bubble arm." They poked a bunch of holes in me and got most of the air out, but for weeks I could move around a sizable air bubble under the skin of my arm. Lots of fun at parties.

And...they didn't fire me. However, I was a required stop for every new hire so I could show them my bubble arm and act as a cautionary tale for one and all, along with the one-armed guy over near the drop press and the three-fingered guy on the table saw.

New Year's at the emergency room for three years straight

Year one...fun with razor blades

New Year's Eve, I am in the basement of my house cutting insulation for pipes. The pipes are above my head. I quickly slice the insulation with my box cutter/ razor blade and immediately realize I have cut the hot water line. The hot water runs down my arm and drips onto the floor. One problem, though—the pool on the floor is red...blood red. It seems I had run that razor blade across all the fingers on one hand. Off to the emergency room.

Year two...using my spine to break the fall

Next year...New Year's morning...stepped out onto our concrete porch stairs at 6 a.m. to get the paper. It had snowed overnight, light snow on top of ice. I took one step onto the snow with my leather slipper, levitated about three feet off the ground, broke the fall with my back and broke off a rib at the spine. That hurt. I would still be there, frozen stiff, if our dog had not alerted my daughter, who came out to inquire why I was lying in the snow in my bed clothes.

The paramedics came to get me and took me to the ER. Gee...it sure looked familiar.

The next day there was an important meeting of the leadership team at work at an offsite location about an hour from my home. Somehow, I drove to the meeting. I have never been in so much pain. Half an hour into the meeting, my boss, Jack Callahan, called a break and pulled me aside. He told me that the expressions of pain, the profuse sweating and the groans were distracting everyone in the meeting. He told me to go home. He then took a look at my eyes and guessed, correctly, that I was also higher than a kite on pain meds. He arranged to have me driven home. I woke up the next morning wondering where I had left my car.

Year three...no goal for Dad, but a nice cast for the broken thumb

Upon arrival at the Emergency Room this year, my wife filled out some paper work for me and the staff entered it into the computer. Soon, the receptionist turned around and asked, "Mr. Hurzeler, is it possible that you have been in this emergency room on each of the last three New Year's?" Indeed, I had. This year, my son had pulled my skates out from under me while I was getting ready to take a shot on goal in our basement hockey game. The fall broke my thumb badly. Three New Year's to remember, and I don't even drink. I'm careful like that.

Blown-out the passenger side window

As can happen to any of us, I had a gas pump explode right next to me as my car was being serviced. I was at the gas station. The attendant (remember those?) had started the gas flowing and walked back into the station. What he and I did not know was that gas had been leaking underground into a big concrete electrical box. Apparently, the equipment down there sparked, the gas fumes ignited and all hell broke loose. It sent a piece of sidewalk and a manhole cover high enough in the air to bring down the electrical lines above us. They ended up just feet from me sparking and jumping around. The explosion blew me from the driver's side of the car to the passenger side and right out the passenger side window, which had been up at the time. Oh, and I was on fire. As I bounced on the concrete, the gas station attendant suggested that I run. Since my hearing was now pretty much gone, I rolled instead. The good news, it was just one blast. The vapors blew up and there was no follow-up fire.

I don't go to that particular gas station anymore. Net loss, my car was toast, my best suit was pretty crispy, and my hearing was completely shot in my left ear, but about half of it happily returned once the law suit was settled. With age and wisdom, in retrospect I promise I would much rather have the lost hearing back than the sizable check that came my way.

I'm not sure how I could have been careful enough to have avoided that mess. Sometimes shit just happens. My wife agrees, at least that's what I think she said. She kind of mumbles.

Ever see the bone from your big toe poking through the skin? I did.

My wife, our kids, ages five and seven, and I all took karate together. Hard style, Japanese-instructed, full-contact karate, which is bare-fisted fighting using fists, feet, knees and elbows to pummel your opponent. We all took the same class. We were lowly white belts. There were people with everything up to and including a black belt in that one class. I think it was family class. Can't fully recall.

One night we practiced forward kicks, the kind you would use to kick some poor guy in the balls, not to put too fine a point on it. After much practice, our instructor had us form a circle and sit down on the mat. He told me to continue standing. He then proceeded to berate the entire class because I...a lowly white belt...was the only one who had done the kick correctly. I was still fairly young and was still in athletic shape, running the hurdles in track meets and able to do the splits. I could kick. He saw that. He wanted me to show everyone how to do it. This is the moment where you would show my head enlarging several sizes—I was singled out in front of black belts and my entire family as the "pro" in performing the front kick.

Our instructor brought out a 200-pound body bag filled with, I think, concrete. He hung it up, had me assume the position and commanded me to attack the body bag with my deadly kick. I charged it like a mad man. Kicked as hard as I could. Hit it right in the nuts.

Now, ideally, the kicker would hit the 200-pound body bag with the ball of his foot. I chose the second position, the one where the big toe is driven deep into the concrete filled body bag. Just the big toe.

It turns out that is a more advanced move than I was prepared to deliver. In my case, the bones of the big toe exited the skin on the top of the toe and brought about considerable pain. I dropped to the mat like a dead man. I threw around my arms, swore, cried and yelled with the searing waves of pain. The instructor informed me that it was not good to show pain. Really? Let me compound fracture his big toe and see how much he enjoys it.

He continued the class with me in it, bloody white bone sticking out of the toe. You may think this is one of my exaggerations. It is not. He had me continue the class. First, he had everyone look for my toenail, which had gone missing. It was nowhere to be found. Next, he basically made the point that nothing would interrupt his important instruction. He had everyone do a quick stretch and THEN he dismissed the class. We went to the hospital for surgery. They found the toenail, shoved way back under the skin. They never found my inflated ego—it was fractured beyond reconstruction.

I lived to get the shit beat out of me another day

I did make a comeback in my karate career. I trained long enough to qualify to fight in a tournament...full contact. I love to fight, always have. Up to this point in my life, I had never actually won a fight, but I sure loved trying.

They matched me with an eighteen-year-old high school boxing champion. We fought three two-minute rounds. In round one he hit and kicked the big muscles (well...not all that big) at the top of both my arms. He just pounded them over and over relentlessly. Pounded them to poi. Round two went a little better for him, as I was unable to lift either arm. He used round two to stomp my legs and knees repeatedly until I could hardly stand. When I came out for round three, I finally scored some points. Unable to use either my arms or legs for offense or defense, I was able to show the judges how well I could take a punch. They stopped round three when my headgear had been spun around so forcefully that I was looking out of one ear hole trying to guess when the next punch would arrive. I came in second in that bout.

That was the end of my karate career. Karate is harder than it looks on TV. However, it was not the end of my injury career.

Beat up on Thanksgiving Day and my dad brings in the culprits at the end of a shotgun...or so he thought

Thanksgiving Day, early. I was about 14 years old. My best buddy, Mike Fayles, and I head down to the beach to go surfing. A car goes by filled with people we think are friends of ours. We wave at them. The car stops, comes back and five guys (whom we've never seen in our lives) jump out and beat the daylights out of me and rough up Mike. I'm still swinging and cussing at them through a lip that is split completely in two when they get back in their stolen car and speed off.

We head to the police station and my folks get a call. My dad asks me to describe exactly what happened. I tell him. Mom takes me to the hospital to be stitched up. Looks like a liquid Thanksgiving for me. Dad disappears. Once I get home from the hospital, Dad calls and asks Mom to bring me down to the police station. We go and find that Dad has, single-handedly, captured the bad guys.

The cops take me into a room with a two-way mirror...very cool. On the other side of the mirror, five of my buddies. Turns out Dad got the wrong guys. How did he capture them? He found a beat-up car with five guys in it that may have fit the description I gave him, pulled up behind it at a stop sign, ran up to the driver's side of the car and knocked on the window. The driver rolled down the window and my dad put the barrel of his 12-gauge shotgun directly in his face. The kids decided to follow his instructions without question. Dad spent the rest of Thanksgiving going to five different homes to personally apologize for his mistake. Mistake or not...Dad was and is my hero for going after the bad guys who beat the crap out of his son. God bless you, Dad.

Ever jump high enough to come down with your body on one side of a cyclone fence and your arm on the other?

My very first stitches were special. I was maybe eight years old. I went over to North American Aviation Recreational Park in Hawthorne to play baseball. I was in the outfield when someone hit a very long drive in my direction. I ran straight at the fence, jumped as hard and as high as I could and caught the ball in the webbing of my glove. A hero's catch for an out.

But not so quick...the batter claimed it was a home run because after I had caught the ball, my momentum carried it over the fence while it was in my glove. The only thing that kept the ball from falling on the ground on the other side of the fence was the fact that I had become impaled on the top spikes of the cyclone fence. My underarm was caught on the barbs at the top of that fence. My feet were a couple of feet off the ground. My arm and glove and the ball were hanging in the air on the outside of the fence. My body was hanging on the inside. Once they got me down, I did not stick around long enough to hear if they gave him the home run.

My parents were called and showed up quickly. They rushed me to an emergency room right at the Los Angeles International Airport. I remember the doctor pulling the wound open enough for me to see the big dark artery that the fence had just missed, then shoving a piece of fat back into the wound, saying that

I was so skinny I needed all the fat I could get. I still have that nasty scar, but I got over the "skinny" problem later in life.

Catching a cue ball with my eyebrow

And speaking of sports, never stand at the end of the pool table when Tom Jacobs is breaking to start the game. My buddy Tom hit the cue ball, the cue ball hit the racked balls and then took flight, flying off the table and hitting me directly in the eyebrow. Knocked me the fuck out. When I came to, my buddies were all still laughing at the sight of me dropping like a rock off a cliff. When I moved my hand from over my eye, they stopped laughing. I was bleeding like crazy and the wound was gaping.

Getting this injury taken care of was not as easy as one might think. Seems that Tom and I had told our parents that we were going to the library. That ALWAYS meant that we were going to shoot pool for hours on end and smoke cigarettes with the boys, but they didn't know that. So I had to wake up my granddad to have him take me in for stitches. Daddy Mac was pretty cool about such things—he would not rat us out and, in fact, gave each of us a beer afterwards, something that any 16-year-old would very much appreciate.

Wish I had a better ending to this story, but when I got home, my parents heard me drive up. They came out of their bedroom and met me at the door to say good night and to find out why the library had stayed open so late. What they encountered was a kid with a massive black eye and a destroyed eyebrow held together by stitches, smelling like beer and cigarettes. Caught by surprise, there was nothing I could do except lie extravagantly. I told them that I had helped a chain-smoking doctor get out of the car he had wrecked before the police arrived to arrest him for driving under the influence. I had injured my eye while breaking the car's side window with my head in the few seconds I had before the car was fully aflame. Dragged him out through that window and saved his life. He later poured some of his beer on my eye wound to sterilize it before he went into his medical bag (which I had also saved) and sewed up my eyebrow. They seemed comforted by my story and thanked me for my bravery. Least I could do.

Tom was later repaid when I exited a breaking wave by kicking out my 9'4" Jacobs surfboard in such a way that it flew through the air and hit him, the fin cutting open his chest like a steak knife. That upset him. He repaid me by waiting until I had grown my first five chest hairs, then one day when I was lying on a flat rock trying to warm up after surfing in the cold Pacific Ocean, he approached me and suddenly reached over and grabbed every single one of those five chest hairs and ripped them out in one move...gone. This may have delayed my puberty by many months, and it really pissed me off.

Death and disaster in big surf

I was surfing at Honolua Bay on Maui in 15-foot waves when I accidentally surfed into an area of lava tubes and rocks. It cut me up badly and gave me a concussion. Most unfortunately, while I was still in the area trying to recover enough to figure out how I was going to paddle my broken board and body to a beach somewhere, enough blood squirting from my hand that I did kind of wonder about sharks, I looked back to the break and saw a local kid run into just about the same area that I had run into, and it killed him...broke his neck. They later brought his body into the medical facility where I was being sewed up. My young kids asked what had happened to him. The doctor didn't even look up. He just said, "He was surfing with your dad."

An aside—this was about 1980 and one of my first encounters with the medical system here in Hawaii and the doctor turned out not to be a doctor. He was a paramedic. I found this out as he was sewing me up, and I expressed my concerns. The paramedic said they had no doctors on call on Maui at that time. He could have me Medivacked to Oahu if I preferred. I did not prefer and he did a great job of putting in about two dozen stitches.

Near death by drowning at Sunset Beach, Oahu

My buddy, Veith Moore, is a veteran big wave surfer. He lived at Sunset Point. We visited Veith and he suggested I join him for a surf at Sunset Beach, Oahu, in good size surf (he would probably call it small surf). He loaned me a short board. I had never ridden a short board. It did not go well. I wiped out and nearly drowned. My wife followed me down the beach as the current swept me away. She finally went for help. Fortunately, at just the moment that I was about to give up, a wave came along, picked me up and threw me on the beach like a sack of potatoes. Veith was very concerned, but we finally did find his board.

Near death at Huntington Beach Pier

Two of my cousins watched me almost die in big surf one Christmas Day at Huntington Beach, California. I was paddling out from the beach near the pier when a large wave let me get right to the top before taking me over the falls backwards and holding me down for three waves. When I was finally let loose from the white water, I swam as hard as I could for the surface. Instead, I swam directly into the sandy bottom. I finally made it up and headed for the beach.

That day was completely fogged in. But it was pretty easy to figure out which way to the beach, as the current and breaking waves were pushing in that direction. I was not sure how far I would have to swim to get to land and I have to admit I was getting a bit concerned.

Half way to the beach, I had about had it. I started looking around for help. As if by a Christmas miracle, there was another guy in the water not too far from me. I swam over to him with my last little bit of strength. Just as I got to him, he turned around, started flailing, and yelled, "Help...I'm drowning!" I told him to flip over on his back and relax. I mentioned that if he even thought about coming over to grab onto me, I was going to drown him right then and there. That seemed to calm him down and both of us made it in.

The cousins thought this was all great fun and wondered if I wanted to go out for another wave. They were from Colorado. They'd never seen a nearly dead guy come out of the ocean before.

Other fun while surfing

There are few things on earth more fun than surfing. Is it dangerous? I don't think I ever heard a true surfer call it dangerous. The sport does, however, present some hazards that surfers may encounter from time to time. Here are a few....

Back when I was a kid, surfboards were huge, heavy and had no leash. They would fly through the surf and air like unguided rockets, destroying whatever they hit. Got my front teeth screwed up enough by a surfboard hit that I had to have my front top teeth pulled and a bridge put in. Next surfboard hit took out the bridge.

Next up is marine life. If you are in the ocean, you are in the home of whatever marine animals happen to inhabit that area. The ones that are particularly injurious to surfers are jellyfish and stingrays. I have had my fill of both; they are no fun. But the ones that scared me the most were the sharks that cruised right below me in clear water. We used to see lots of those in California. Big sharks, but mostly harmless leopard sharks and the like. Still, if you are a nine-year-old kid sitting on your board with your feet dangling in the water waiting for a wave and your see something as big as your board cruise directly under your feet, you pull those feet up onto your board and maybe take the next wave in.

Surfing at Bluff Cove in Palos Verdes, California, in the winter meant paddling WAY out to catch a wave. It might also mean that you would encounter seal, seals that would want to play, or pester you, or even try to take a nip out of you. Fun...up to a point. However, when you see a seal porpoising toward the shore at top speed, it is time to take a look over your shoulder to see what might be right behind it.

One winter day I saw a half dozen seals fly by me and turned to look out to sea. The point of land we called Indicator was way off, but I could see a fleet of small black and white buses porpoising toward us maybe a half mile away. We immediately knew those small buses were orcas...killer whales. They were a rare sight...thankfully...but well known to cruise through during the winter gray whale migration period. And they like seals...for breakfast. In our wetsuits, we looked a lot like seals.

All of us in the line-up took off on the next wave. We never stood up, just held onto the sides of our boards and paddled hard at each place the wave reformed (there were typically three breaks when the surf was good-sized), so we could make it to the beach fast. We all made it and then cowered up against the cliff with the seals as the orcas patrolled the bay. Pretty exciting.

My dad and I spotted a lone orca in the surf line at about 22nd Street in Redondo Beach one morning. It was stalking a small kid playing alone in the surf. Dad stopped the car and I ran straight down the ice plant (a low-growing succulent) covered hill and onto the beach. I launched into the water and grabbed the kid, who started screaming and thrashing at me. I don't blame him because I had no time to explain what was happening. I dragged his uncooperative self onto the dry sand only to be joined by his screaming mother. I did not say a word to them...I just pointed. The orca was still there. I then ran back to the car, got in and, in true Hurzeler fashion, we drove home...nothing further said. By today's standards, should have taken a selfie.

Going head-to-head with a tiger shark

Our boat harbor near Kona is well known for the tiger sharks that live at the entrance and sometimes swim into the harbor. Those trips are fairly predictable in the summer months, tied to tide changes and fishing boat activity. I like to photograph tiger sharks, but I am just a little hesitant to do so on my own while snorkeling. So...I came up with a plan.

The idea was to stake out a spot near the entrance and quietly slip into the water with a crinkle bottle (an empty water bottle that sounds like a fish in distress when squeezed), said bottle in one hand and my camera housing in the other. I would use the rocks there as my backstop so nothing could slip in behind me. I could also use the rocks to get the heck out of the water if the tiger shark did not want to play. Brilliant really.

So one summer day I man my station. Here comes the biggest of the tiger sharks, our well known Lavern...about 14 feet. Wait a minute, Lavern is being accompanied by four other smaller tiger sharks and....what is that?...a couple of manta rays. This is beginning to look like a National Geographic cover shot for Donny.

I got very excited and scrambled over the rocks toward where I planned to get in the water. Didn't even look like I would need to use the crinkle bottle, Lavern was headed right toward me. I had to speed up to get there in time...shot of a lifetime ahead!

Running on wet rocks in wet slippas (flip flops) is not always as wise as it might seem. I stepped on a green rock and went flying, head first, directly toward Lavern. She never saw me coming. My camera housing hit a rock hard and shattered into pieces. My body hit a rock hard and crushed things I need, like ribs and fingers. My head either hit Lavern or glanced off a rock near her.

Lavern and her posse made an immediate exit right back out to sea. Me...I just tried to stand up. I had ruined the shot. Hurt myself. Broke the expensive camera housing all to hell and broke it so completely that the fisheye lens inside the housing was now ninety percent broken off from the camera and just hanging there. A disaster.

I heard a man's voice coming from the lawn above me. I turned my bleeding head toward the sound and looked at him without speaking. He did the speaking. I know the guy...he owns a boat that is tied up right there. His only comment, "Dumb shit." Seemed about right.

Sharks and killer whales sound scary, but it is things like sea urchins that get you

If you are not familiar with a sea urchin, think of a black tomato covered in six-inch-long, needle-sharp spines. My buddy, Doug Elden, and I went surfing at Rock Pile near Waikiki. We rode a wave or two and I was paddling back out for more. A wave hit me and drove me off the back of the surfboard feet first into the reef. Fortunately, the reef was protected by the biggest sea urchins ever. I got dozens of sea urchin spines in both feet, The spines stuck out of my feet five or six inches. You can't pull them out. I had to break them off at the skin and paddle into the beach.

On the beach, I hobbled over to a lifeguard who took a look at my feet and asked me if I had peed on them yet. What? "Yo, brah, you got to pee on those things. It will break them up and make you feel mo' better, yeah." Now, I am no medical expert, but this was a serious injury and, for some reason, I decided that the lifeguard might not be giving me the best medical advice. Off I go to the hospital, literally walking on the sides of my feet.

Honolulu has some great medical facilities and terrific doctors. I needed some help right now, because the next day I was going to be on stage in front of a lot of people. I was speaking at a convention. The doctor saw me right away. Looked the feet over carefully and asked me, "You did pee on them already...right?" I think the bill was $120 for this advice.

All of the sea urchin spines dissolved eventually, except one. It became infected and very painful. I needed surgery to remove it. I had the surgery done in Illinois. That sea urchin spine is still taped to my medical chart there and I've been told that the doctor has shown it to several of my friends. He doesn't get a lot of sea urchin wounds in Chicago.

A couple of shark stories to keep you up at night

I live in Hawaii and I am in the water almost every day. People here regard sharks as just part of the landscape, the true residents of the sea, with us as the trespassers. Some even afford them spiritual reverence. It is hard to tell a story about a shark encounter without someone saying something affirming like "just part of nature, bro." Shark stories do not impress us much in Hawaii. That said, I am going to tell you two shark stories that did impress me...one in California long ago and one here on the Big Island a few years back. The first is in the form of an actual short story I wrote about our encounter and it goes like this...

Curt was my next door neighbor in Huntington Beach, California. We were both about thirty-five years of age at the time, married, had kids and big deal grown-up jobs. Despite reality, we both thought of ourselves as seventeen-year-old surf bums.

Curt and I had a trio of poor surf options. We could get up at some horrible hour and surf before work. We could surf only on the weekends and fight the crowds. Or...the pier is lit at night and we could surf next to it all night long. We often chose option number three...night surfing.

One night we arrived at the pier to find the fog right up to our eyeballs. We could hear the surf and guessed that it was pumping. We waxed up our boards and concluded our warm-up routine, leaving one can of Coors unopened for when we came in. We paddled out in the diffused light of the pier, a bit spooked, but anxious to go.

The first hint of trouble was a loud "Oh shit!" from Curt. He was just in front of me and in no time at all, a breaking wave, Curt and his board were all over me and my board. We ping-ponged together through the pilings of the pier.

Back on the beach, we assessed the damage. My board now sported a major tail ding. His board was missing. All he had left was the ankle strap and about a foot of leash tubing. The tubing looked as if it had been cut by a knife.

We looked for fifteen minutes in the dark and could not find the board. I finally told Curt I had an idea...he should look down the beach while I caught a few waves. I launched while he was still speechless.

Two pilings out, I found Curt's board. It was leash-hooked on a piling. I paddled over, pulled it loose and paddled it back to the beach. I yelled for Curt, who quickly returned and was amazed to have his board back in relatively good condition. He told me he no longer considered me an asshole. We launched again.

This time out we tried the right side of the pier. That way, if a wave hit us it would take us away from the pier and not into it. After a few minutes of determined paddling, we made it out to the surf line.

The waves were bigger than we expected. The peak was just beyond the light of the pier and hidden in the fog, but we knew where to find it. Just as we got into position a clean-up set rolled through. It was everything we could do to get over the first wave...we pushed through the lip of the feathering wave at the last possible moment. We kept paddling, probably another twenty yards or so out. By now we could not see shit—dark of night, no pier light except as a glow to one side, no light visible from the beach or parking lot.

I think it was I who suggested we paddle out another fifty yards or so to be safe while we talked over our options. We needed to come up with a plan to get back to the beach...in complete darkness...in big and building surf. Our beer buzz was long gone.

"Hey, only eight more hours to sunup," I joked. Curt was not amused.

Curt was the first to get hit. His left leg was smashed so hard by a creature that it threw him off his board. As soon as he realized he was in the water with his attacker, he started to swim. Curt was an ex-lifeguard and still a strong swimmer. He looked like a windmill in a hurricane as he headed toward the beach.

Before I could say anything, I got hit...hard, but a glancing blow. Now both Curt and I were in the water.

There was no talking, no yelling...hell, I couldn't even think. There was only no-shit-I-am-headed-for-the-beach swimming.

I did not make it ten feet before I felt a major tug on my ankle. I pulled that ankle in toward me as hard as a human could pull. My ankle came flying in, as did the surfboard that was still attached to it...hitting me right in the face and crushing my nose.

Great...I am now in the water with my nose bleeding like a faucet, God knows how much blood was pumping out of the leg the shark hit, and it is dark and right in the middle of the impact zone. Life could not get much worse. Turns out it could....

I flailed around with my arms to grasp my board, thought I could either try to prone ride it in to the beach or protect myself from the next shark attack. What I found was the jagged area of the board where it had earlier hit the piling. I was now bleeding from my arm as well as my nose and leg.

I just lay there on the board waiting for a wave or shark to destroy me, whichever could get to me first. Curt was nowhere to be seen. The roar of the ocean drowned out all other sounds. It was dark and getting darker every moment. There was no longer any glow from the pier or from anywhere for that matter.

The wave caught me first. I was sideways in the impact zone when it hit me. I was instantly off my board. I felt the leash snap and, seconds later, my board slammed into my ribs. And now my board was gone...have a good day, Don.

I tried to remain calm. Best lesson my dad ever gave me...when things get really bad, get really calm. I got as calm as I could, given the wild surf I was in, the bleeding and the shark. I did actually think that the shark would be too smart to get trapped in the surf line, so I was probably no longer in danger from him. As beat up as I was, I started to feel like I might make it.

Every surfer knows this feeling...after a bad beating in the water finally feeling the sand beneath your feet. No better feeling ever! I was safely ashore. A quick look and I saw I had no major injuries and no bleeding from where the shark hit my leg. I was going to be okay.

I found Curt. He too was okay. We looked each other over, expecting to see a shark tooth stuck in our skin somewhere or a long tear in the leg we had not noticed previously, but found nothing. We were truly okay.

I found my board. Curt never found his...on its way to Seal Beach in the dark. I also found my way to the emergency room to get sewn up, happy to be alive.

Curt and I talked over that session dozens of times. To this day, we do not know for sure what hit us...never saw it and it did not leave a mark. Could have been a shark...could have been a bonita running into us at full speed or some other large fish. Whatever it was, it ended our night sessions.

Story number two is worse...

I have a love/hate relationship with the surf at Waipo Valley on the Big Island. I love Waipo Valley and approach it with respect because it is a very culturally important part of our island for everyone and especially for the Native Hawaiian people. The hate part comes from two things, the first is the road down to the valley floor... one small lane with a huge drop off on one side. I cannot drive it. I always ask my business partner and friend, CJ, to drive it for me. I sit next to him with my eyes closed. God forbid there is someone coming in the opposite direction because one of you will then have to back up to a small pullout point, my worst nightmare. The second thing is the ocean at Waipo Valley. It has a black sand bottom and often a very strong current pulling you down the beach. The black sand makes it difficult to impossible to see what is beneath you, especially when we are normally there before sunup to photograph sunrise down the tube of an incoming wave.

One morning we arrived on the beach at Waipo Valley well before sunrise. There was enough light in the sky to see that the surf was roaring. We figured that the best way to get out to the surf line was to jump in the river that runs through the middle of the beach and ride it out. Sounds ok, but that river is really cold and I know, from long experience, that sharks like to patrol the debris line to see what the river might run their way—perhaps an easy meal of a dead pig or such. That last bit of danger never seemed to blip the screen for CJ or Nick, my fellow surf photographers that day, but it sure made me edgy.

It all went to plan. Soon we were in the line-up, spread out about twenty-five yards from each other just waiting for the sun to rise so we could get our shots. That is when I heard Nick shout—and not a fun kind of a shout. I looked over and he was headed out to sea...arm extended...behind a dorsal fin and a thrashing tail fin. A tiger shark had grabbed his camera housing and taken off. Nick's arm was still attached to that housing by a leash.

CJ and I both swam toward him as hard as we could, but before we could get to him, the shark let go of the housing and disappeared. We checked Nick over, not a scratch. We checked over the housing...a few scratches but it was still functioning. Time to get the hell out of there.

Nick and CJ do not think like I think. Nick said...and I quote, "Hey, we got up at 3 a.m. to be here, drove down the sketchy road, jumped into a cold river to get out here and now we have probably scared off the only shark within a mile. It is only ten minutes to sunup. Let's hang out, get our shots and get out of here then." CJ quickly agreed with him and swam off to his former position. I tried to hold back my tears as I did the same.

Two minutes later a beautiful wave came my way. By now there was enough light to actually photograph it. I moved a bit to get in just the right place. The wave was about five feet high, but it jumped up to maybe eight feet when it hit the sand bar. When it did that it was only ten to fifteen feet in front of me...the moment I would normally pivot and take several shots down the tunnel of the wave as it passed over my head. Except this time the ENTIRE face of the wave was filled with tiger shark....one big-ass tiger shark that I estimated to be about a hundred feet long (later revised to only ten feet by CJ and Nick). I dove under the wave and the incoming shark, surfaced, put my hand on my head with the symbol of shark as I yelled "big boy!" to CJ and Nick and then turned all my attention to getting the hell out of the water. I made it without incident and CJ and Nick immediately followed. We watched that shark work the surf line for the next half hour and then headed home.

The one other time I had been bumped hard by a tiger shark at Waipo, it turned out to be just CJ messing with me. I mention it because on that occasion, as I turned toward my "attacker," my hand instinctively squeezed the trigger of the camera and I caught CJ's smiling face in an image that I look at often. So, as soon as I got home I opened up my images to see if I maybe got lucky again. This time... not so much. What I did see, however, was a big swirl underneath me in the frames a minute or so before the shark wave hit. Again, no telling, but I am guessing I had that tiger shark beneath me at one point, in the black early morning hours of Waipo Valley.

Fun with marathons

Marathons have been a wonderful source of injury and pain. I took off my shoes after successfully completing the Pikes Peak Marathon—you run to the top of a 14,110-foot mountain and then back down...26.2 miles on a goat trail with huge drop-offs in several places—and out fell four toenails. The pounding those toes took on the steep downhill parts of the race took a nasty toll.

The Los Angeles Marathon left me with just a bit of my big toenail hanging on. It was a bloody mess. My future son-in-law, Joe Stanczak, and my daughter were along to provide support for me on that run. After the race, the three of us went to Cabo San Lucas, Mexico. Joe could not keep his eye off that horrible looking toenail...like looking at a car wreck. So I broke up a tortilla chip to just about the same size as the toenail, waited until I knew I had his attention and started playing with the hanging nail. When I felt like he was just about to barf from watching this activity, I yelped a bit and flung that tortilla chip right into his lap. Joe looked like he had just had a rattlesnake thrown on him. Still makes me laugh.

More fun with marathons...nipples bleeding, upper inside thighs rubbed raw, blisters the size of marshmallows and all the fun that comes from running through bat guano.

That last one...the bat guano—I had the good fortune to run a marathon in a cave in the Netherlands. There were bats in the side tunnels and there must have been bat poop on the floors. And I ran like bat poop. Turns out that the Grotten Marathon (which has now changed quite a bit) was for elite runners only. That would not include me. Few of the runners spoke English. The entire race was in a cave, except fifty yards of each mile as you came out one tunnel and went into another. It was dark in the tunnels. You had to wear a helmet with a light on it. I clung to the walls as the runners repeatedly passed by me yelling something that I took to mean "get out of the way, old man." Finally...no more runners...just me. They had all finished and gone home. The race organizers sent someone in on a bike to encourage me to quit. I informed him I would finish and finish I did... well after everyone else. The only person left at the finish line was the young lady with the finishers' medals. She was there to give me a kiss on both sweaty cheeks and a medal. I looked up...the finish clock was gone. Fine with me...it was my slowest marathon ever. I did beat one person. She turned an ankle and had to be carried away.

Well, at least golf is safe...not!

Not even golf is safe for me. I recently drove my golf cart, at full speed (the only speed I know), into the stump of a tree that had been taken down a few days before. There was just enough stump left for the grass to cover it and create a land mine for me to hit. I hit it right on the axle of the golf cart. My friend Gerald Chiddick and I flew through the windshield. I made it through the windshield after first spearing my ribs on the steering wheel. Broken ribs for me. Screwed up shoulder for Gerald. My best drive of the day...completely wasted.

Gerald has had other problems with me and golf carts. He is not fond of snakes. I like them. We came across a rattlesnake on a Florida course. I tried to chase him down, but he got away. I did find another that was trying to bite me or someone and I believe I used a nine iron to end his run. I thought for sure that Gerald would want to see him, so I curled him up and placed him on the floorboard on his side of the cart. Turns out that Gerald did not want to see him. Later that evening, we both listened to a report on the local TV about a golfer from that course being medivacked to the hospital due to a rattlesnake bite. I'm guessing that Gerald is pretty much through with me on the golf course.

I ran track and field as a kid...

Running track was lots of fun. I was a sprinter and a hurdler and I was pretty fast. Fast enough that one of my competitors came across three lanes to step on my foot at the end of a preliminary race to try to put me out of the finals. His spikes went completely through my foot...holes in the top and bottom. Quite a sight. I beat the daylights out of him in the finals.

On another occasion, I passed the fastest hundred yard dash guy in the league as he and I anchored our quarter mile relay teams. He reached up and broke my nose with his fist and baton. I still beat him. Even more fun, his dad and my dad got into a fight in the stands over the incident. Loved it.

My college roomy, Jim Frost, was an excellent high jumper and a big guy. One time he and I went fishing on Irvine Lake in Orange County, California. There may have been alcohol involved. I stood up to cast my fly. It hung up on something. I pulled and pulled until Jim's big hand grabbed my shoulder. Seems that I had sunk that fly into his neck and all you could see of it was a tiny bit of feather. I bet that hurt.

We went to the hospital and they cut the fly out of him. Next day in practice, by sheer coincidence, Jim stepped on my foot. That was good for about a dozen stitches. On Friday I told the coach I was ready to help at the meet in any way I could...take times, carry starting blocks, keep an eye on the equipment...you name it. He named it. He wanted me to run all my events. I mentioned the dozen or so stitches in my heel. He mentioned my scholarship. I ran. I believe that they only had to replace about half of the stitches.

Enough about my careless life. I could tell you about a fractured neck that resulted from diving into a pool, breaking my elbow while racing a neighbor kid with me running backwards, fracturing my arm falling off my skateboard, running my finger through the saw when I was a butcher's assistant, falling down an entire flight of concrete stairs after being introduced to a drink called a Velvet Hammer, cutting my tongue nearly in half falling out of a tree, having a steel door fall on my head...concussion and stitches to follow, falling over hurdles and landing on my shoulder on a crushed granite track, setting up a punch press wrong and then having the punch explode, hit me in the chest, blow me across the aisle behind where I was positioned in front of the press, and knock me out against the wall, and a dozen other events that had me in stitches...but I won't.

But there is one recent injury worth mentioning. Happened the day before Easter two years ago. I was out in decent-sized waves photographing surfers coming down the barrel at me. The session was going really well. I guess I got a little too confident and managed to get just a little bit out of position...enough so that a wave picked me up and slammed me to the sand like Hulk Hogan. My camera housing, with camera, probably weighed ten pounds. It was attached to me by a surf leash so I would not lose it. That housing hit the bottom, got torn out of my hand so hard that it took off a couple of fingernails, extended out to the end of the leash and then came flying back at me like a cannon ball. It hit me at the hairline (which these days is WAY back on my forehead) and tore a giant gash in my head. I sputtered to the surface, staggered to the beach and reached up to see if I could stop the bleeding.

Once I was on the beach, a lady ran up to me and told me she was a trained medical professional and that she could evaluate the wound for me. I told her that would be appreciated and bent over to show her the injury. I heard her dry heave. She was still dry heaving when I lifted my head up. That kind of tickled me somehow and I said, "I am going to take that as an indication that I should show this thing to a doctor." She nodded and I was off to the parking lot.

Once I got in my car and backed out, a car full of tourists (and by the way, I love tourists...without them Hawaii would have virtually no economy) pulled up alongside me and asked if this was a safe beach for their children. The wound was on the side of my head away from them, so I said, "Yeah, pretty safe. You might want to be a bit careful in the surf today." At that, I turned the injured side of my face toward him and I sure as heck wish I had a photo of the reaction of everyone in that car—it was priceless. I am guessing they are still telling that story.

My own story does not end there. I drove directly to an urgent care here in Kona. The doctor came out to see me and assured me he could fix me up with a few staples to the noggin. "Sound good to me," I said. "Let's have at it." He told me he had to clean the injured area first, which seemed unnecessary since I had washed it out at the beach shower, but he was in charge, so I was in for a wound cleaning. He asked his assistant for something to numb the area so he could clean and staple it. The assistant informed him they had nothing in stock. The doctor, who was a visiting doctor and working there for the first time that morning, said, "What do you mean we have nothing to numb it with, we are an urgent care, for God's sake." The assistant informed him they had run out, but would have more by Wednesday.

The doctor informed me I would need to go to the local hospital for treatment. I informed him that the local hospital currently had a scabies infestation and that I was not about to go there with a head wound. I told him to have at it. He told me it would hurt like hell. Give it your best, I told him. He did. It hurt like hell. And now the moment I had been waiting for...the staples being driven directly into my scalp. He told me to hold on...this was going to hurt. He was right about that....the staples hurt even more than the cleaning. He asked me if I was okay. I could barely reply, but I told him to proceed. He then informed me that he had some bad news, the first staple had not gone in correctly and he would have to take it out and start over.

Once my legs regained enough strength for me to stand and possibly exit with my freshly-stapled head, I turned to leave. The doctor asked me to wait a minute and disappeared. He came back with a prescription. I'm hoping for heroin or something even stronger. Nope...it was made out for Office Max, and it was for a staple remover. I looked at him and said, "You have to be shitting me." And he was. Only smile I had managed since seeing the tourists' reaction.

CHAPTER SIX

Putting Myself in Danger...Then Waiting for the Magic

Two more pretty amazing stories to tell you...the first features me coming as close to a violent death as I could ever imagine. In the next I am an observer as one of my best friends falls—and nearly dies.

When I was 14 years old I lived in a beach community in Southern California. Life could not have been any better. We surfed all day and camped out at night. The weather was warm. The waves were occasionally decent. I had no job, no responsibilities and very little in the way of good sense.

My sister, Pam, has her birthday in August. The day of her birthday, I decided to hitchhike up to the shopping center with my best friend, Mike Fayles. It was hot as heck and I recall wearing shorts, a tee shirt and either no shoes or flip flops. We got a quick ride to the center, I bought Pam some nail polish and a card and we headed home. This little outing gave me an opportunity to smoke a cigarette or two, buy an ice cream at Thrifty's Drug Store for less than a quarter and generally poop off the afternoon. Quite a nice way to spend part of the day when you're 14.

On the way home, Mike and I ran into a snag. We sat in the hot sun for a very long time trying to get a ride home. No one stopped. Finally, in desperation, we saw our chance for a ride. An 18-wheeler came lumbering up the steep hill hauling two hoppers full of gravel. The heavy load and the steep hill caused the truck to just creep past us. I looked at Mike, he looked at me and we both started running. We chased down the truck and managed to hop onto the flat areas above the rear tires...he on one side of the truck and me on the other. We had our ride.

Now Mike and I were not rocket scientists in those days. And, much like the algebra class I failed several times, I had only been able to figure out part of the equation. The other part, the how-are-we-going-to get-off-this-truck part, we did not even consider. So, we slowly rode up the hill, happily waving at cars as they passed by.

When the truck got to the place where we wanted to disembark, we both noted a bit of a problem. We had hesitated just a little too long and the truck was picking up speed. Now what?

Mike answered the question right away and jumped for it. This was almost sixty years ago and I may be a bit confused about what happened next. My recollection is that Mike's hand got caught on something and he was unable to let go of the truck. What I do recall clearly was his running along behind the truck. Mike on his best day may have been able to run 15 miles an hour. I believe the truck was doing about 30 miles an hour. His feet hit the ground every so often and pieces of flesh flew off his foot, his knee or whatever touched the pavement. Either I was able to free his hand or it came loose on its own, and Mike went tumbling madly toward the curb, a bloody, beat-up mess. My best friend was looking like he was very seriously injured, nearly dead, and there I was, speeding away from him at 30-plus miles per hour. I have never felt so helpless.

As for me, heck, I had just seen what happened if you jumped. My decision was easy—I was going wherever the truck wanted to take me. When the truck came to a full stop, I would jump off and run for it. If that happened a mile down the road, cool. If that happened half way across Los Angeles County, also cool. I would figure out a way to get home and I would be in one piece. I sure hoped that Mike was going to be okay.

Riding backwards on the wheel cover of an 18-wheeler that was now going about 45 miles per hour is not as safe as it might sound. No seat belt. Heck, no seat. No protection from the sun, the wind, the flying debris...nothing. Just my skinny butt bouncing around and me holding on for dear life. Oh, and those heavy hoppers filled with gravel...they were built on a rail system that allowed them to move back and forth some, right next to me.

I recall waving at the cars behind us. I was no longer smiling. I was waving to get their attention. I wanted off this damn truck and I was willing to take my medicine—in the form of angry adults—to get off. I hoped that one of the cars would pull up and someone would yell at the truck driver to tell him what was going on. That is just about the time that some real alarms went off for me. I noticed that none of the cars was able to catch up to or pass the truck. In fact, the truck was passing the cars.

We were on a two-lane (in those days) road that curved around the side of the hill where we lived. Parts of the road ahead were steep and there were many turns. The road eventually terminated at a stop sign at the bottom of the hill. Past that stop sign was a field. Past that field was a several-hundred-foot high cliff and then a plunge into the ocean. I began to think about the road ahead.

The next two things I heard put me on full red alert. The air brakes on the truck sounded like an air hose with a hole in it. Lots of air sound...no braking sound. And, I heard the truck driver sounding the horn repeatedly. My guess, we were doing well over 65 miles per hour by now. I recall thinking, "I'm fucked." And...I was. The truck had lost its brakes.

By now, the truck driver, who had no idea I was on the back of his vehicle and had his hands full anyway, was running the truck into the side of the road cut to try to slow it down. Guess which side of the truck that happened to be. You got it...my side. He would hit that cut of rocks, cactus, plants and dirt and it would be right there...an inch away from me. It blasted me like a sand blasting operation. Covered me in a cloud of dust. And the horn kept blaring. And the rocks kept flying. And my 14-year-old mind tried to figure a way out. I quickly came up with a plan.

Part one of my plan...prayer. I asked for forgiveness, prayed for my soul, begged for help and made promises to God that I could never keep.

Part two of the plan...get as far away from the upcoming wreck as possible. First jolt I was going to push off as hard as I could and that would be that. Not much I could do after lift-off. I knew I would be in God's hands. That was all I could hope for. This was not going to end well.

That jolt came just moments later. I knew we were coming up on a big curve. What I did not know was that there was a liquor delivery truck right in front of us doing all it could to outrun us. We hit that truck hard. The next nanosecond was me flying though a dust cloud and then complete darkness. It was all over for me.

I woke up many minutes later, possibly a half hour later. I was a long way from the wreck. I had landed in a freshly plowed field, just past a huge boulder in a bunch of local vegetation. I stood up....big pain. I looked myself over. I had on a tattered pair of shorts, no shirt, no shoes and there was blood everywhere. No one was running over to help me, so I started slowly walking back up to the wreck. But wait...for reasons too stupid and embarrassing to bring up, I remembered that I had a condom and a pack of cigarettes in my front pocket. I knew I was headed to the hospital or morgue. I figured I could take the heat on the cigarettes, but that condom was going to be hard to explain. What was a 14-year-old kid doing with a condom in his pocket? I can assure you...nothing. I carried it around because I was pretty much delusional about sex in those days. The old "condom in the wallet"... that was me.

I ditched the condom and the cigarette pack and started hobbling out of the field and up the road. I found out later that I had broken my pelvis, but I managed to walk quite a distance on that broken infrastructure.

When I did arrive at the scene of the wreck, a short stocky guy was looking over the side of the road at the destroyed liquor truck on the hillside below. My mind did not comprehend anything about that liquor truck. What I was focused on was that 18-wheeler with two hoppers that was lying sideways across the road, smoke pouring out of the engine and gravel spread across half an acre, and the short stocky guy with his back to me.

I tapped the guy on his shoulder and he turned around quickly. He took one look at me and nearly screamed. He asked me if I had been standing on the side the road. I asked him if he was the driver of the gravel truck. He said he was. I told him I had been hitching a ride on the back wheel cover and had been thrown away from the truck on impact. The tough-looking truck driver tried to form a question, but his eyes rolled up into his head and he passed out at my feet.

The next person I saw was some kind of a paramedic soldier guy from the Nike Missile Base that was located about a quarter mile from the wreck site. Here is what I recall of him...he was African-American, he seemed to be in more shock than I was, and he wanted nothing to do with trying to attend to my wounds. I don't know his name or anything else about him. I do recall that I asked him if I was going to be okay. He said, "Take a look for yourself," and held up the side mirror that had broken off the truck. What I saw was the area around one eye pretty much erased from my face and a trail of abrasions that left raw meat all the way down one side of my body. I did not look even remotely like I was going to be okay. He said he was going to get me someone who could really help me...and I am thankful he did. He called for police and an ambulance and I was eventually on my way to the hospital.

I've only thought about that trip down the hill on a truck with no brakes about a thousand times since then. I really cannot think through any sequence of events that would result in me living through it. I should have died there, age 14, my only accomplishment in life being two small medals for track won during my freshman year. My parents could have collected my broken-up body, my never-used condom, half a pack of Marlboros and a bottle of nail polish for my sister and driven back home to live out their lives wondering what I could have been had I not been so stupid. I'm guessing that condom would have given them a mystery to consider as well.

The aftermath of this whole mess...

Mike got really badly cut up and mangled by the road rash. I'm not sure how the skin on his knees ever healed, but it did. He has lived a long and productive life and we are still the best of friends.

My sister got her nail polish with no card and no brother around to wish her a happy birthday. In fact, this whole episode kind of erased her birthday celebration from the calendar that year. Pam...sorry for messing up your special day. I promise I won't do it again.

The truck driver made it through the ordeal with no physical injuries. The truck was a total loss. The liquor truck was also a total loss. The only time I ever saw the driver of the liquor truck was years later outside a courtroom. I was to be his only witness—he was suing the driver that bumped him off the cliff. He told me he was really counting on me to testify on his behalf and that he hoped the lawsuit settled before it went to a jury. I asked why he was concerned...this was an open-and-shut case. He said he was worried because he had done time in jail for murder and thought the jury might not be sympathetic to him. Oh, great...a convicted murderer was betting everything on my testimony. Happy to say, they settled out of court.

As for me, I still remember almost every moment of that day. I remember the ambulance ride to the hospital. The long delay after the X-rays and the asshole doctor who handled the reading of the X-rays as if it were a joke "And the answer is...no skull fracture." I lost sight in my right eye for a few days, but was told that it would return when the swelling subsided. It did. The broken pelvis healed. The only lasting physical manifestation of the accident was a nasty scar I still own above and around my right eye.

But there was one more thing...

I spent a night or two in the ICU. The guy next to me...a Mr. Watson...was there because he had had a heart attack. We talked a bit before we fell asleep. He seemed pretty concerned for my mashed-up face and inability to see out of the one eye. He was in good spirits despite there being lots of tubes and wires attached to him. Mr. Watson was a heck of a nice guy. So off to sleep.

In the absolute middle of the night I awoke to a commotion. The very first thing I saw with my one good eye was a needle that may have been a foot long being plunged directly Mr. Watson's heart. That sight, or the sedative they gave, put me right back to sleep. In the morning, Mr. Watson was gone...no Mr. Watson, no bed...just an empty space. Mr. Watson had had a heart attack in the night, this one massive, and he had died. Try processing that information as you lie there all alone in ICU, a scared and hurting 14-year-old with one good eye.

So God...as I have mentioned so many times before, thank you for the bonus time that has made up the majority of my lifetime. Thank you for getting me out of a completely impossible situation. I apologize and ask for your forgiveness for whatever promises I made that I am sure I did not keep. Thank you for Mike living through this debacle. Thank you for the lives of the two drivers. Thanks for the opportunity to meet Mr. Watson. And thank you for my not having to be the one and only witness for the convicted murderer...I would hate to have disappointed him in any way.

I am thankful for every single day of my life. Each one is a gift. It could have all turned out very differently and I know that I am one lucky guy. Stay off of trucks without permission and don't carry stuff around with you that might create a lot of unwanted conversation were it to be found on your dead body. Life is good.

C.J. Kale...now you see him, now you don't

This particular event happened on January 29, 2012...not that I am keeping track. The Kilauea volcano was erupting at the time, sending lava downhill to a sea cliff and then over the sea cliff and into the sea. The area at the bottom of the cliff was accumulating new land from the fresh lava, which got bigger and bigger. Typically this new terrain would get so heavy and the waves would erode it so much that cracks would form and it (we call it the delta) would suddenly break off into the ocean. If you happened to be standing on that piece of real estate at that random moment, you died...crushed by the rock, burned by the hot lava still inside the delta and then drowned by the ocean. The last guy who died on a delta collapse here was famously heard to say "oh shit" as his last words.

We had not been out on the lava for a while because the consensus was that conditions were ripe for a delta collapse. That is why I was surprised to get a call from CJ and Nick inviting me out for a photo session.

"I thought we agreed it is too dangerous out there right now" was my instant reply.

They agreed, but said that the lava was entering the sea at many points along a broad front and we should be able to pick a safe spot once we got out there.

I told them we were leaving the island in two days for a signing with my most recent book, *The Way Up: How to Keep Your Career Moving in the Right Direction*. I really couldn't take a chance on getting hurt. I thanked them and wished them luck.

Ten minutes later the phone rang again. Seemed they felt it would be much better to have three of us out there in case something did go wrong. Would I please reconsider? Again, I declined.

The next phone call came just five minutes later. They promised to have me back home by 10 a.m. Would I please come along? I looked at Linda, closed my eyes and said, "Yes." They picked me up at around midnight.

Now, CJ and Nick are pros at being out on the lava. Me...not so much. Oh... and they are in their 20s and 30s, and me...well, I was 63 at the time. I can outpace them walking on a flat surface any day of the week, but on the lava they blast ahead and I always trail behind just hoping to be able to stay in contact.

On this night, the moon had gone down and it was black as the inside of a cow out there. It was also much tougher terrain than I had experienced in the past...lots of ups and downs and jumps across cracks in the lava. After about a half hour or so, I could see the lava flowing into the sea along a section of the field...quite a sight.

I was just scared enough out there to do everything I could to stay right behind them. CJ took the lead. Nick was behind him by a couple of feet and I dragged along in third place, some several feet behind Nick. All of a sudden, I heard CJ say, "Lights up ahead." That is not always good. You can't be sure who those lights belong to or what they might be doing out there in the middle of the night. Better to stop and watch to find out what they are up to. Unfortunately, CJ did not do the "stop" part. He took one more step forward while trying to see what was going on well in front of him, and he just plain disappeared. All I saw was a black and white tee shirt that looked like it was just sucked into the earth. No sound...just that very sick image of CJ dropping into God-knows-what to land God-knows-where, very likely dead or broken into pieces.

Nick and I fell to our knees. We really didn't know what had just happened. All I knew was that I was now kneeling with my head hanging over a huge crack in the ground and my light pointing straight down into it. At the bottom of the crack, some 25 feet down, was a crumpled CJ, lying on his side, eyes closed, not moving and looking quite dead.

Nick briefly went just plain nuts. He kept saying, "Oh my God," and jumped all around the sides of that crack trying to find a way to get to our friend. I was afraid he was going to join CJ at any moment and tried to get him to calm down... which he did immediately. We then heard a stirring sound and looked down to see CJ with his head lifted up toward us. His immortal words were "Brah...I broke my fucking leg." Happiest words I've ever heard. I thought he was dead, and broken legs can be fixed.

Next step, how do we get this broken up 200-pound guy out of a 25-foot crevice without doing him or us more harm? There was no good answer. We finally asked him if his arms worked, if his other leg worked and if his neck and back seemed all right. We also looked him over with our lights to see how badly he might be bleeding. Miraculously, CJ was in pretty good shape, save the bone sticking out of his sock.

Here is how we saved him. We told him he was going to have to crawl out himself. There was no help available anywhere. We had no safety equipment with us or in the car (never said we were a group of geniuses). He would have to move from rock to rock until he could get to within about ten feet from the top and then we could probably pull him out by his backpack. And...that is exactly what we did. CJ did the scrambling. Nick did the heavy lifting. I kept the scene well-lit and tried to keep everyone focused on the task. Looking back, a pretty good team.

I think we were all amazed when we finally got him out. We looked him over and talked about things like "going into shock." CJ had had lots of emergency medical training while he was in the Navy and he felt he could control his situation. We tore apart an expensive tripod and constructed a brace for his compound fractured leg. He wasn't bleeding too badly. He had his wits about him and wanted to get moving before his adrenaline wore off. I took a few pictures of him and the crevice to document the event, and we then set about the task of getting him to a hospital. Imagine how sick we are that one of our first instincts was to get some pictures. Sick puppies indeed, but we are all glad we got them. If you ever want to see what pain looks like, check out the picture of CJ that I have posted on my website. Major league pain.

We had a lot of camera equipment with us...a lot. While Nick worked on CJ's leg, I grabbed all three camera bags and headed back to the car. That gave me about 90 pounds of gear to lug over the lava field...middle of the night...scared to death...not entirely certain where the car actually might be. I think that Nick and CJ quickly figured out that I was going to be in big trouble and soon Nick was catching up with me. I was very happy to see him and very hopeful that we could both find the car and then find CJ again. We succeeded.

When we got to the car, Nick found the medical kit. It consisted of...and I am not kidding...two ibuprofen and a bandage. We laughed that off and headed back for CJ.

Our first efforts to move him were to grab him by his legs and arms and just lug him. That did not work...at all. Next, we told CJ once again that he was going to have to do most of the work. We would support him on either side and he would have to hop on his good leg across the lava. And that is exactly what we did. At one point, one of the three of us stumbled and CJ's weight dropped onto his bad leg. I can still hear that pain come blasting out of him. We did not let that happen a second time. One side note...CJ is shorter than both Nick and me. His arms were up around of our necks, pulling down on them hard for maybe 45 minutes. It took both Nick and me a long time to get over the damage done to our necks, but there was no avoiding it.

I will never forget the burst of hope I got when we saw our car just a hundred yards ahead. Even better, a couple was nearby and I yelled to them for help. They came over, assessed the situation and calmly asked us the safest way to get out to where the lava was flowing. They offered no help or sympathy at all. I offered no directions. Complete assholes.

Getting CJ safely into the car was one of the highlights of my life. There were long minutes where I didn't know for sure if we were going to be able to get him to safety and all the other possible "help" strategies we could think of seemed problematic at best. There is no cell phone coverage out there, no landmarks, no good places for a helicopter to land and none of us really knew if CJ had other injuries that would put him in danger of dying. But, he was now safely in the car and we were on our way to the Hilo Medical Center.

When we did get cell phone reception, we used the map service to help us find our way to the hospital. It worked perfectly, except it delivered us into the jungle miles away from the actual hospital and said, "You have arrived at your destination," the only good laugh of the night. After a couple more missed turns, we found the medical center.

By now, CJ was in massive pain. He is a tough guy, but he had been injured hours ago and he was really hurting. I took another picture of him as they pumped in the meds. CJ was now euphoric. Nick and I enjoyed watching him right up to the point that the doctor said he was going to pull on that foot and see if he could get the bone back in place. Nick and I exited stage left. We suspected that CJ's smiling was about to come to an abrupt end.

Somewhere along the way, the hospital staff got the wrong idea that I was both CJ's dad and a doctor. I'm not sure what caused them to come to these conclusions, but I did nothing to correct them. They then gave me direct access to his X-rays and put me into a consult with his orthopedic surgeon. I remember looking that doctor in the eye and making him swear to me that he had the skills to put CJ back together well enough for him to continue to earn his living doing dangerous things . He promised me that CJ would be all right and it gave me confidence that CJ was in good hands. Several hours of surgery followed...steel plates, lots of steel screws in the bone...complicated stuff. CJ came through in great shape.

I was in the recovery room with my peers...I mean the doctors and nurses... when they rolled a quite screwed up CJ into the room. His first question to me: "Are we still on for Ruth Chris Steak House tonight?" I had promised them a great meal there on our last night in town. I was scheduled to leave for the book tour the next day. I informed him that the dinner was off for now. I think he asked me that same question another dozen times. By the way, the doctor busted me when he caught me trying to read an X-ray upside down.

As we were leaving Hilo, we passed CJ's wife, Amanda, as she was arriving. I wouldn't see any of them again for four months while I was on the mainland trying to sell a few copies of my book. We kept in touch by phone, but CJ is one of those "yeah...I'm doing great" guys...so I wasn't entirely sure how he was doing. The doctor had told me his greatest fear was an infection at the site where the bone came out through the skin. On my first day back on the island, I went to Lava Light Galleries to see CJ. He wasn't there. Will was there. Will runs the gallery when the boys are out shooting. Will is closer to my age, he has lots of degrees and smarts and he has been all over the world. When I asked him how CJ was doing he told me straight out that he was worried as hell. Told me the leg was infected and bright red and hot. I could tell he was shook up by it. It shook me up as well.

When I saw the leg I about puked. It looked horrible. And CJ was limping badly. A pretty damn scary time. Skip forward another year...CJ is healed. His limp is almost completely gone. And...CJ, Nick and I hiked out on the lava again just last week (I wrote this part about a year after the accident.). It was a huge test of CJ's ankle and we found out he was back big time and ready for action.

And the oddest part of all this...aside from the assholes who wanted to know the safe route to the lave flow while we struggled with our broken-up friend, is that the lava quit flowing into the ocean at almost the exact time that CJ hurt himself and it really didn't returned until he was healed. It waited for him. I think the lava likes the way CJ makes it look in all of his pictures. And if you don't think that there is a presence to the lava... a life force somehow imbedded in it...then you haven't spent enough time out there watching the miracle of new land being created. And I am forever thankful that this story has a happy ending. I'm always in favor of a happy ending.

Now, if you spread everything I've told you about my being uncareful for over 73 years, it doesn't sound as bad as you might have thought just reading about it all at once. I guess the lesson I learned is...oh, heck, I haven't learned any lessons at all from this stuff. I've always played hard and never much thought about "what if." Unfortunately, the "what if" came along quite frequently for me and I paid the price. I'm cool with all that...water under the bridge...price of admission...what doesn't kill you makes you stronger. However, what I have learned late in life is that our actions have an effect on others.

Imagine being my poor parents, for instance. They told me thirty years after the fact that on Christmas Day the year I was 16 they sat above the Palos Verdes Cove as Eric Wolff and I stupidly paddled out into the biggest surf I've ever seen there. There was no one else out. No help on the beach—or anywhere. The surf was breaking WAY out in the ocean. And my parents sat there watching. They told me they wanted to be able to tell the Coast Guard where to look for our bodies. Shame on me for putting them through that agony.

And now I am 73. I was six miles out in the ocean off Hawaii last weekend free diving with very large sharks. No cage, no shark stick...just my camera housing for protection, some very large swim fins for kicking at the sharks and a couple of friends in as much danger as I was. I'm thinking that the second edition of this book will have some new entries.

CHAPTER SEVEN

The Pivot From CEO to Lava Man

Lava has fascinated me from as early as I can remember. A large part of why we retired to the Big Island of Hawaii is the fact that this place has one of the world's most active volcanos. Kilauea's lava flow has been a source of great joy and deep sadness over the years. It has paused for the moment...and I am thankful for the blue skies that have now returned and yet I can't wait for it to start flowing to the surface again in some remote area—we are all one over plan for a lifetime on seeing it erupt in a neighborhood. The 2018 Puna eruption was an event of a lifetime and one I wish I had never experienced, but more about that later.

My wife and I started coming to Hawaii in 1969 or 1970 to visit her grandparents, who lived here at the time. We traveled to the Big Island and saw our first lava flow up close and personal...and it hooked us for life. Later, I brought my aging folks over to the Big Island on their 65th wedding anniversary and hiked them out to the front of the flow, thankfully a very easy hike at the time. We also took my mom out to Halema'umu'a Crater at a time when it was splashing lava all over the crater floor and shooting lava well up into the air. We took her there when she was about 95 years old...took her out there at 3 a.m. so she would not have to deal with the crowd. She said it was the most beautiful thing she had ever seen.

Moving to Hawaii and our first lava boat adventure

I retired from my real job at age 61 in 2008. We lived in Chicago at the time and at the beginning, I played golf until my hands bled from June to September. My handicap went from a 9 to a 12...so I guess it wasn't lack of play that was keeping me from being successful at golf. In October we went to Australia for a month. In November we leased a place in Kailua-Kona, Hawaii, and moved there for several months.

In January 2009 we heard about this guy with a boat who would take people out to where the lava was hitting the sea on a very remote part of the island. We checked into it and found it was a pretty unique operation. First, you meet someone in the middle of a tropical jungle area at 3 a.m. and they guide you to where the boat will launch. That meeting place was two hours away from our house, so we rented a place in Pahoa for the night (much closer to the launch site) and learned all about coqui frogs. They sound like they are whistling loudly...kind of fun to hear one, but you hear thousands, so we didn't get much sleep that night.

When we arrived at the launch site we were surprised to see the boat trailered on dry land. After an orientation in the dark by our captain, Shane Turpin, we were instructed to board, in the parking lot, via a large step ladder. They backed the boat over to a small launch ramp at Pohoiki Park. This is when my concerns clicked on. I had surfed Pohoiki and knew that there was no way around the surf line—the boat would have to drive right through the middle of it. Why was this a concern? Because I could hear the surf and judged it to be six to eight feet and there was no long run up to it. By the time the captain got the boat turned toward the sea, we would be just about in the surf. It was at that point that the boat hand told us all to turn off our lights because the captain needed his night vision—the boat had no lights to see what was coming. Oh dear!

That started the second scariest boat ride of our lives. The eighteen-year-old kid across from us prayed out loud for the entire trip out. Everyone on the boat got seasick and threw up, except Linda and me. We would have thrown up, but our throats were tightly closed from fear and we could not. It was a heads-down-pray-with-all-your-might, completely dark and rough ride out to the lava flow, which was about 45 minutes away. The deck hand walked up and down the aisle as if it were a normal trip on a ferry and offered his throwing up customers a tasty grocery store donut for their breakfast treat. No takers.

When we arrived at the flow, it was one of the most magical moments of our lives. The lava flow had created enough of a curve in the coastline that the ocean surface was protected from the swell and wind—it was like glass. The lava was dropping over a forty-foot cliff directly into the ocean. There was steam all around and that steam reflected the red hot lava and gave the whole scene a surreal look. Lava would periodically explode as it hit the cold (cold compared to the 1600-degree lava) sea water and shoot up into the air, looking and sounding like fireworks. Jaw-droppingly beautiful.

The guy in front of me on the boat turned and said, "I would rather be here than anyplace on earth." I replied, "Not me. I want to be one of those guys on the cliff." I pointed up to the cliff where two guys were standing directly next to the flowing lava and photographing it as it fell into the ocean. He said, "Well, one of those two guys is my son." And so the next morning, Linda and I were standing at that very same spot with that son, C.J. Kale, and his then photo business partner and great friend, Nick Selway. The photo on the cover of this book was taken by CJ on that night...with Linda hanging onto me for dear life. We had on respirators to keep us from frying our lungs. We had those yellow slickers on to try to keep the sulfuric acid off our skin. The ground was shaking and CJ made us stand as still as possible until that plume of red gas framed our heads. We were scared to death—for good reason. The next day when we went back out there, that spot had fallen into the sea. It was also on that day that I found out how unbelievably bad I was at photography and how amazingly good CJ and Nick were. And so our photo adventures began.

By the way, CJ and Nick were young and working with very little capital in those days. They drove us over to the lava flow in Nick's "Exploder," a ghettolicious old, beat-up Explorer with seat belts you TIED across your laps. They were tied so tight on the trip out that we had to be cut out of them, then we had to stop at an automotive store to buy new ones on the way home. Not sure how any of us survived those early days.

Shane Turpin and his lava boats

Shane got really good at his lava boat service. He ended up getting a second boat and eventually a third and made a big-time business out of it. We loved going out with him. We always took the first boat of the day, usually leaving around 4 a.m., depending on the time of year. When we would arrive at the flow, Shane turned on Johnny Cash singing "Ring of Fire" and it was on! We had days when we got out there and all hell was breaking loose, so we shot photos until our arms could no longer hold up our long lenses. Other days we got out there to find smoking, dark lava piles with absolutely no lava flow going into the ocean...a wasted trip and a big disappointment. It was not like Shane could call ahead to check conditions; he was the guy whom everyone else called because he was always the first guy out there.

Was it dangerous out there? Could be. Shane was as careful as you would want him to be and he certainly knew what he was doing. By the time he got his new boat running it had four 250-horsepower engines on the back and an aluminum hull, so he could move positions quickly...a good thing considering that pieces of lava could be floating in the water. Lava is filled with gas and it breaks into pieces when it hits the sea. Many of those pieces float and spin as they de-gas, eventually sinking to the ocean floor. But they are hot as hell and you really would not want to be floating around out there in a fiberglass hulled boat.

We know a guy who did just that. He had a tiny boat and some tourist offered the guy money to take him out to see the lava dropping into the sea. (That is the story as told to me...might have it wrong and I'm not going to mention his name.) Our friend took him up on the offer. He did not have a permit to take people out there, but no matter, off they went. Once out there the tourist saw one of those floating pieces of lava and asked the captain to see if he could get a closer look. The captain got a bucket and fished that lava out of the sea and then poured it out on the deck. Apparently it melted right through the deck and hull and found its way back into the ocean. This left a large water fountain in the middle of the deck and the boat soon sank. Our friend and his passenger managed to get picked up by a nearby boat, but his boat was lost and his tour operations came to a permanent halt.

On Shane's boats, we saw lava hitting the sea in many different ways. The amazing lava hose that lasted for months...a 65-foot-high stream of rapidly moving liquid lava that shot out from a broken lava tube on the cliff and arched into the sea. We saw lava benches build up at the bottom of the cliff, get large and larger until they covered acres of new land and then abruptly broke off and fell into the sea...that is the nature of the beast. One of those broke off right in front of us with no warning and Shane expertly maneuvered us out of trouble. Our guests, Sue and Ray Lamoureaux, will never forget that moment—they were closest to the bench and took some nice video of the action. There were tornado-looking things (vortexes) that formed in the steam on a regular basis due to the heat differential between the lava and the ocean. These vortexes would be swirling all around us. Things popped and shot high in sky and if it was still dark out, they looked like fireworks. We heard things out there that would startle us and we sometimes couldn't figure out where the sound came from. It was always exciting, always interesting and always different out there. We loved it.

To get his passengers ready for this adventure, Shane always gave a safety and expectations lecture to everyone. It would be impossible to give a clearer safety briefing/warning to the people on that boat than Shane always gave. We used to stand to the side and quietly laugh during his briefing because it was so honest, direct, clear and stern. He would tell people not to go...that there were dangers out there that he could not control...especially the lava and ocean conditions. (We can vouch for that...it could be a scary and rough ride out and back.) He would try to scare them into not going, and on the rare occasion when he succeeded, he would give all their money back without penalty. He wanted to protect everyone, but especially the old, the infirm and anyone who had a back problem or was pregnant. We have watched him sort out a few people on the spot and tell them they could not go...too dangerous for them. It was a safety briefing unlike any other I have ever witnessed...just about impossible not to understand that you were about to embark on a dicey adventure. All that said, I know of only a couple of relatively small injuries to passengers over the years...mostly from passengers not hanging on or ignoring the captain's instructions.

I also know that Shane's boat was his pride and joy and that he took his role as captain very seriously. I found this out for myself a few times when I suggested he maneuver the boat in certain ways so I could get a better photograph and he let me know in no uncertain terms (he is a sea captain after all) that he would not put others in danger so I could get my stupid photograph (his term for stupid started with the letter F). The chances he took out there were a bit like a magician's tactic of misdirection. He made it look more dangerous than it was. He had 1000 horsepower to work with, a sturdy double-hull design, a metal hull and thousands of hours of experience. Shane was and is someone with whom I would and have trusted my life in a dangerous situation. And I know that during the Puna eruption, a lava explosion did hit his boat and injured several people. I am so sorry that he ended up that one time in the wrong place at the wrong time and that people were hurt. I especially hope that the young lady who was hurt the worst will fully recover. God bless them all.

And God bless Shane. Shane gave us memories for a lifetime. He is a good friend, someone I respect and very much appreciate.

CHAPTER EIGHT

Hiking Out to the Lava Flow

There are five kinds of lava hikes.

The National Park or County Viewing Area lava walk

This is the kind of lava hike I took my 80-some-year-old folks on, where the lava was close to the road and moving very slowly. Park Rangers are around to keep you safe and walking areas are clearly marked with cones and florescent tape. Lots of people who tell you they have hiked out to the lava took this hike....and it was Linda's and my first lava hike many decades ago.

The lava hose road hike

This hike was several miles long. You walked out to the Lava Hose, a 65-foot-tall fountain of lava that exited a broken lava tube on the side of a cliff and arched down like water being released from an emergency relief valve on a dam and into the ocean. It lasted for several months in 2017. You could also ride a bike out there. The road is a graded road that connects Kalapana with Hawaii Volcanoes National Park. It was built in case a volcanic flow cut the Puna District and Pahoa off from normal exit routes. A good and fairly flat, straight volcanic gravel road.

On the Kalapana side of the Lava Hose hike, a tent city sprang up with people selling or renting supplies for the hike, including bikes. We had our own bikes, but chose to hike most of the time, as the road was rutted and gravelly and very soft in spots. Not a day went by that we did not see someone crash their bike and get ground up by the lava gravel. Also, the first time I loaned my bike to Nick to take out there, someone stole it while he was taking photographs over on the cliff. He called me to apologize. I told him that I thought I knew a crackhead over there who was in the bike-stealing business and directed him to look in his back yard. He did, and we got our bike back.

So, the Lava Hose hike was relatively safe UNTIL you got to the cliff. The cliff was in no way safe. Cliffs peel off over time and drop down onto the lava bench or into the sea. If you are on that cliff at that moment, you die...and several have over the years.

I would guess that 90 percent of the people going out to the Lava Hose were either visitors or first-time cliff observers. We watched them do some of the dumbest things I have ever seen in my life. It is only by pure luck that a number of them were not killed. Selfies from the very edge of the cliff right next to the Lava Hose were the major stupid activity. It was not long before the National Park people came in and put a halt to it. They taped off an area and then patrolled it, arresting offenders. We thought the restriction was too conservative, but we are not the brightest bulbs on the string, so I will not criticize them. Most of us who were out there on a regular basis ended up saving at least one person from certain death.

In my case, I watched a Swiss guy walk right out to the stupidest possible place to be near the Lava Hose, where he set up his camera. I took pictures of him with flocks of parrots flying over his head...EXCEPT those were not parrots, they were lava bombs that landed around him like carpet bombs. He never noticed a one. I had to go drag him to safety. Asshole.

My second save was not an asshole...in fact, it was a friend. Nick and I hiked out with a couple visiting from Oregon. We met them at the photo gallery and they asked if they could join us on our next hike out. We said yes. It was 3 a.m. when we arrived at the cliff. Nick took the guy and moved forward of my position. I took the gal and we set up with a good view of the Lava Hose. I set up my tripod and camera quickly, then I turned and checked on the gal. She had moved some and was now in an area that I considered extremely dangerous. I asked her to move. She politely told me that she was fine where she was and had a great view. No time to be nice, so I said curtly, "That was not a request, that was a demand. Pick up your stuff and move over here behind me right now." This came off about as nasty as it sounds and pissed her off. I was quite sure that she was going to move her stuff and go get her strong, young paramedic husband to straighten me out. I was half right. She did move immediately and did move to a position right behind me. But before she could head over to grab her husband, the entire area where she had been standing collapsed into the sea, some eighty feet below. It shook the cliff so hard that we fell to our knees, covered us with dust. When the dust cleared, we both stood and she said, "Well, I am listening to you now." Sometimes you just get lucky.

The next day, Nick and I took them to Kua Bay. The surf was pounding and I gave them a big lecture about how dangerous the surf was and how people had been killed by it. After a few hours, both Nick and I had to leave. They would stay on to enjoy that beautiful beach. As I left, I warned them again.

Not long after we left, the husband, Tommy, looked out to the surf line and spotted a guy floating face down. He and others rushed out to save the guy. They got him to the beach and Tommy did all he could to revive him, putting his paramedic training to good use, but the guy was already dead.

Tommy called me later that day and told me what had happened. He mentioned they had to return home the next day and that he would appreciate it if I kept any thoughts on the safety of their flight to my damn self. He did not want to have to worry about me going three for three.

The oddest moment ever on the Lava Road Hike was the morning that Nick hiked out a gallery customer from Germany. He hiked him out to the cliff to an area where there is no vegetation or building of any kind for at least two miles, just fairly new, black, cooled lava on a cliff some eighty feet above the ocean. It was well before daylight when they arrived and set up their tripods. As the German guy placed his camera on his tripod he started yelling and waving his hand. Nick lit him up with a flashlight to see what was going on. A rat had climbed up the tripod and clamped onto the guys hand....probably smelled remains of the power bar still on the guy's hand after his quick snack. Amazingly, he shook the rat loose without it ever breaking the skin. Gave that guy quite a story to tell when he got back home and sure gave me a good laugh when we met later for breakfast in Pahoa.

The spookiest lava cliff story....CJ, Nick and I hiked out to the ocean entry (the place where the lava flow dropped over a cliff into the ocean). It was about 3 a.m. because we wanted to be there for sunrise, the very best time to photograph the lava flow. It was the longest hike we had ever undertaken, perhaps five miles out over rough lava (before the road had been cut). We got out there and set up our tripods and cameras and were about ready to begin our photography when we heard a sound above us. We looked up to see a tall, thin black woman in flip flops (we call them slippas here). She was crying. We asked what was wrong. She said she had hiked in from the National Park side, a hike even longer than ours, had run out of water, felt dizzy and confused, and her slippas were worn out...she could not walk on them any longer. First thought...slippas? How the hell did she make it this far over rough lava in slippas?

We told her to sit down. We gave her some of our water and a power bar or two to eat. We told her not to move, but to rest for a few minutes as we got the shots we had hiked so far to get. She thanked us and agreed to stay put. I told her that I had duct tape with me and that we could use my shirt and the bottom of her slippas and the duct tape to fashion some kind of shoes to get her back to our car and then we would drive her back to her car. We promised she would be okay and we would take good care of her. She nodded her head and we went back to our cameras. That was the last we ever saw of her.

When we finished shooting, maybe ten minutes later, we turned our attention to her. She was gone. By gone I mean...completely disappeared. We could see a long way in each direction and inland as well...and she was nowhere to be found. We shouted for her...nothing. Carefully looked over the shoreline below us...nothing. Looked for cliff line cracks she might have slipped into...none. She was GONE.

We have no idea what happened to that lady. We read the paper each day for articles about missing persons...but there were none. We sure hope she is alright. A complete mystery for all of us. By the way, she was such an odd-looking person to be way out there, dressed as she was, that I took a photo of her. I will post that photo on the website associated with this book and you can see that this was no ghost...this was a distinguished-looking woman in a very odd place at a very odd time.

The regular lava field hike

The third kind of lava hike is the one we did most of the time. We would start out in either Kalapana or Hawaii Volcanoes National Park and hike for anywhere from a mile to five miles to get to the front of the lava flow. At that time, the lava was spilling out of the Pu'u'O'o vent and flowing down a wandering path to the pali. The pali is the steep drop-off that takes the lava from a couple of thousand feet up the mountain down to the coastal lava fields that eventually spill out into the sea, a stair-step process covering a dozen miles or more. Our regular lava hikes were across that coastal plain. The hike was from where you start to where you see the closest red glow of the running lava. The area between those two points was highly uneven, up and down, old and new lava flows...smooth lava rock, jagged lava rock, cracks in the ground to watch out for, hot spots to avoid, areas where gas accumulated...enough to kill you under the worst circumstances.

CJ, Nick, Linda and I did dozens, if not hundreds, of these hikes. Sometimes we had clients with us from the gallery. Other times we took out friends or relatives visiting from out of state. We hiked out a camera crew or two so they could do coverage of the volcanic eruptions or highlight the adventures of CJ and Nick. Most were fairly safe and uneventful, with a half hour or so of fantastic photographic opportunities tucked in the middle as our reward for all the hard effort of getting there. But a few were downright life-threatening.

Linda and I hiked my editor, Bob Gorman, his wife Mariann and some family members out there. Bob is like me...part of the Social Security set. He has been my editor on several previous book projects and served as a consultant on this one. The hike was a stretch for him, but he made it. Once we got to the hot spot, I noticed that he and his family had found a high spot and were waiting there for us to do our photography before we headed back. I learned later that it was also right at the edge of their comfort zone, being that close to the running lava. Every time I see him, he mentions that trip—that trip had some magic for them.

We did the same with our daughter, son-in-law and two of our grandkids....the day before Christmas...out to an amazing lava flow. Glad they got to see it.

As you saw in the story about CJ falling down the crack, the biggest danger out on the lava field is normally just slip and fall. Any fall can be dangerous. Lava is sharp as glass and hard as rock. We hardly ever made a trip out there when one or more of us was not cut up. Our rule was...if you don't think you will bleed out, we keep on going. That applied also to the time I not only cut myself up, but knocked myself out in a fall. Shake it off. Try to stop or slow the bleeding. Keep on keeping on. Leave the house at about 1 a.m. and be back home by noon or so. Those trips were totally exhausting.

CJ and Nick had a couple of habits that I loved and hated. First one...the false encouragement move: "Hey Don, the flow is just up over that ridge." The flow was never just over that ridge. "Ten more minutes" was another...it meant twenty minutes to an hour more.

The second tore at my ego...but was much appreciated. On the way back, Nick or CJ would stop for a rest. One of them would distract me and the other would steal my heavy backpack. He would then head off towards our car many miles away. I know I am the old guy and can use a little help, but this one was an ego crusher. I would protest and they would fire back with "we are all going to fry to death out here if you don't get moving." And they were right...it got hot as hell out there once the sun came up and we did always need to move faster...something I could not do with a twenty-five-pound pack on my back. I learned to just take it and be grateful.

Every time we made it back to the car, it felt like we had completed a marathon. I could barely move. My back hurt. My shoulders hurt. My feet hurt. Whatever I had cut that day hurt. Hurt locker for sure. But we got the photos. I loved it.

Not every day out there was the same. We had a day when we got caught without our gas masks and a storm came in and steam covered us quickly...steam filled with deadly gases. We had to strip down and cover our nose and mouth with our clothes, bury our heads in the volcanic shards of glass on the ground and pray for the storm to pass quickly. Once it passed, we brushed ourselves off, coughed for a while, put on our clothes and hightailed it out of there. That afternoon I got a call. It was my friend Bruce Omori. He asked me if I listened to Tupac. I told him I loved Tupac. I asked him why he asked. He told me it was because that was what was playing when he found my expensive phone lying in the lava field just feet from the flowing lava. Bruce got the phone back to me...would not accept a reward....just questioned my taste in music.

Another day we encountered a Japanese visitor at the launch point for our hike. We asked him where he was going and he told us in pretty good English. We told him it was too dangerous to go where he was planning to go and that he needed a lot more water and supplies to have any kind of a chance. We urged him to not go. He thanked us and went anyway. His rental car was still there when we returned...and for many days after. I don't believe he was ever found.

We have another rule out there. It is called the Run Rule. If someone yells run, you do not look around or ask why...you run. I got to try that rule out with one of our visitors. After a long and difficult hike, we could not find the running lava. We found lots of lava that was still quite warm, but none running on the surface. The guy we hiked out was completely freaked out by the whole experience and started to cry. I think CJ couldn't stand it and said he would head off to scout the area and would be back...we should sit tight. More crying on our visitor's part. We had told him about the Run Rule...and he had paid attention. All of a sudden, as he and I sat there alone on top of a still warm, but empty, lava tube, something shook the ground mightily...like an earthquake or a stampede or a landslide. Whatever it was, I was not about to stick around to find out the cause. I shouted "run" and we both took off. We stopped about a hundred yards away and looked and listened to see if we could identify the source. We could not. After about ten minutes, we returned to our designated spot to wait for CJ. By the way, this seemed to stop our visitor's crying. He was now shaking violently...quite an improvement as far as I was concerned.

In another ten minutes or so, CJ returns and I am very happy to see him, as is our visitor. I told him about the sound we heard and speculated that it was a lava tube collapsing. CJ informed me I was right. It was a lava tube collapsing (maybe even the one we were sitting on). It had collapsed as he tried to cross it, taking him down into the still-warm tube about six feet... uninjured and in a place where he could pull himself out. Our visitor began crying again. At that, we gave up our quest for the lava flow, accepted defeat and hiked back home. We never heard from that guy again.

Other encounters out there were just plain silly. Like the woman we came across about two miles out from the launch point who was hiking in alone with her dog. The dog was in a wooden cage strapped to her chest. It was a mid-sized dog. What the heck?

Or the morning I abandoned an exhausted Linda before sunrise and took off on a solo mission (never a very smart thing to do) to get to the front of the flow before sunup. It was a long way off and there was a very dangerous area of gas between me and the flow. However, I got there in time for sunrise and was happily taking my photographs, completely alone. Then I heard a female voice. Turned out to be two young ladies approaching the flow. They told me that they were going to change their clothes. My first thought was, do I have the right lens on for this event? But what they really meant was that they were going to put costumes on... over their clothes. They did. Within minutes they looked like two dinosaurs out on the lava flow. Then they began to mimic a dinosaur fight, T-Rex vs. whatever kind of dinosaur the other one was. I noticed a guy with them, who was filming a video of the fight. Since they were right next to the 1600-degree lava, in full and flammable costumes, I figured it was just a matter of time before I would get that wish-list "dinosaur gets barbequed by the lava" shot that every professional lava photographer hopes for. No luck. They did their video and escaped unharmed. I got some cute shots of them and gave them the prints on metal. Unique for sure.

Twice I came across international visitors out there who had taken off their shirts to burn holes in them so they could show their friends back home how brave they were.

I want to write about the gases that accumulate on a lava field for a moment. They are dangerous as can be...killers. Two or three times I have been nearly taken out by them. Once I entered an area that had a big gas accumulation and barely even noticed it or was so distracted by the heat of the lava flow around it that I ignored it. Next thing you know, I am on one knee wondering where I am and what happened. That also happened to my buddy Steve Goppert while we were out there...except I think it was more the heat than the gas that got him. He recovered and made it back to the car okay.

My worst one was a night CJ and Nick decided we would hike about a mile across very active lava flows to get to the other side so we could then crawl down a cliff and they could get in the ocean to do wave photography next to the flowing lava. They failed to mention most of this to me ahead of time.

When you get to an active lava flow at about 3 a.m. and look across it to see river after river of lava flowing across the coastal plain to and then over the cliff, one would think you would stop at the first river and take your photos. At least that's what I thought. CJ explained to me that there was a vantage point on the other side of those flows that we just had to reach. I asked him when the helicopter would arrive to take us across those active flows. He told me that we did not need no stinking helicopter, that we could carefully pick our way across those lava rivers and make it to the other side without a problem. Every bit of reasoning I could summon told me that he was just plain nuts and not to listen to him. However, I certainly did not want to sit on this side of the lava all by myself in the dark waiting for them to maybe return...so I followed them.

Holy shit it was hot. That kind of hot dehydrates you faster than you can re-hydrate and we only had so much water with us...a lot, but you never have enough in these conditions. Then we put on our gas masks. That should have told me there was real trouble ahead, but I actually thought those fancy gas masks would protect you from anything...not quite the case, as it turns out. Lastly, I noticed that they left me in the dust. This was unusual for them, as they always watched out for the old guy. Not so much this time. They slipped into high gear and flew across the lava. I continued at my old guy pace and was soon on my knees yelling for help. The gas had me and I could neither stand nor breathe. They yelled back that we would all die if they came back for me and that I had to get up off my fat ass and start running. I found the mention of death to be a motivator and I struggled to my feet and ran as fast and as pitifully as my old legs would let me. I made it to the other side. I was not a happy camper.

Once we were on the other side of the flows, they asked me how I was and checked me out for any real damage. I passed the test and we put down our packs to rest for a moment. It was then that they told me why we were there. We had come to this spot because they thought they could climb down the cliff and into the ocean to do wave photography right next to the lava flowing into the sea. I thought that perhaps the gases had ruined my hearing and asked them to go over that plan with me one more time.

Right off the bat, I hated the plan. I hate it when they get in the ocean right next to the flowing lava. It is a stupid and dangerous thing to do and I love these two guys...I do not want to see them killed while I'm videotaping. Second, I hate heights...hate them. To scramble down the face of a steep cliff, in the middle of the night, carrying a heavy backpack and a tripod, on a crumbling lava cliff I did not even want to stand on, much less climb down...insanity. But Nick told me he had found a safe and easy route and that all I had to do was to place my feet in each spot he placed his feet....and then he started down the damn cliff.

Nick's first step turned out to be onto a recently-vacated lava tube...still warm but no active lava in it. It immediately gave way under his weight and his leg sank in up to his groin. It took him about a minute to get his leg out. His comment: "Maybe over here would be better."

I actually have no idea how nor why I made it down that cliff with them, but I did. Next thing I know, I am standing on the world's most beautiful brand-new black sands beach while my idiot partners are putting on swim fins and placing their cameras in surf housings (where did those come from?).

CJ is the first one in the water. He jumps in and disappears for about one full minute....gone. Nick and I keep looking at one another. My thought...he got sucked into an underwater lava tube and we will never see him again.

But...up he pops. He mentioned that the current had pulled him down twenty-five feet or more...and then he goes about his business of getting his shots. Nick is the next in and does a little better. But, as you will see if or when you go to the website, he is actually shooting shots below sea level...you will have to see the photo to understand it...it is a weird, weird place to be in the water.

I was supposed to take photos of them and shoot some video. At this point in my photographic career, I was just plain not very good at photography and even worse at video. I am still no good at video, but I learned a lot that morning that helped me become a much better photographer. First thing I learned, never shoot in "Auto" as the camera might select an extremely high ISO for you...like something over 20,000. To say that many of my photos from that morning are a bit grainy would be an understatement. But I did fine once the sun came up.

Then our friend Shane came along in his boat. He was surprised to see Nick and CJ swimming around the lava and yelled to me to ask if I needed anything. Yup...I needed water and lots of it. The ocean gets deep immediately in that spot, so he was able to bring his boat in almost all the way to the beach and toss me all the water we could ever need for the trip back.

At some point, after the sun had come up, I shook myself out of my state of total fear and actually wandered over right next to where the lava was dripping onto the beach. I got some interesting shots and realized that very few people in the world had ever had the opportunity to see what I was seeing.

When CJ and Nick got out of the water, they had cuts all over them. Lava, when it hits the water, turns to glass shards or sand. The glass shards had cut them up as if they had been in a knife fight. The water was so acidic that they had a very uncomfortable hike back and then a long drive to Hilo to find an outdoor shower to wash the acid off.

I think CJ and Nick successfully did wave shots from the water next to the flowing lava on five occasions. I was with them for two. Both times they failed to tell me what they were up to. Both times I thought they would die. They did not die and we all got some great shots and CJ and Nick got to be on the Today Show live to discuss their foolishness.

And I can't leave this section without mentioning our friend Sean King... King of the Moonbows. Sean was a larger-than-life guy...big, loud, smiling, fun and a terrific photographer. His moonbow photos were some of the best ever. A moonbow happens in Hawaii at certain times when there is a full moon and moisture in the air...looks like a regular rainbow except you see it glow brightly in the middle of the night. Sean died out there on the lava fields. He got caught in an area of gas buildup. He was leading a group of visitors on their first-ever lava hike. I really don't know the details, but my guess is that he got them to safety, but paid the price himself. Whatever happened, this world lost a terrific guy and the rest of us will never forget him. God bless you, Sean.

The lava hike up the pali

Speaking of Sean, he had some video of a solo mission he did up the pali, with him in a kipuka and a river of lava flowing past him like the mighty Mississippi.

Sean met up with us at the 7-11 in Pahoa at about 3 a.m. We told him where we were going. He told us he was headed up the pali. We wished him luck. That night he posted his video. The pali is the steep part of the hill as the lava wanders down from the Kilauea volcano toward the ocean. It is a difficult climb up, some of it over rough a'a lava...lava that looks like it has just been plowed up into jagged rocks. The kipuka is an area of trees or vegetation that has been spared by previous lava flows. These spots may be a little safer than the surrounding area because they are probably raised up a little so the earlier flows went around them. However, during the course of a decades-long eruption, virtually all of the kipukas get covered over in lava. On this night, Sean was in one of the few remaining kipukas and right next to a raging river of lava. Scary as hell and he was there all alone.

For all the reasons I just mentioned, I rarely hiked up to the pali. I hiked to the base of the pali many times, but really only climbed up the pali on two or three occasions. They are hard work and dangerous and pretty exciting. And there are terrific photos to be taken up there.

On one of those pali missions, we hiked out a couple of German visitors. I was with CJ and his family and the two visitors. We left the family at a safe spot and the four of us continued on...WAY past my comfort zone. The area at the base of the pali that day was fairly recent new lava and crunchy as heck. Every step was on something that felt hollow and warm...not a comforting feeling. I wanted to stop and go back a dozen times, but kept on going. We finally made it to the hot zone and found my old friend Yvonne, plus John Tarson and a half dozen others, already there.

CJ and I climbed up the pali with John and took some photos. I am sure CJ did not consider it dangerous. I know John just considered it another day's work. However, it was dangerous. Lava was dripping and flowing all around us, rocks were falling, the surface was sharp and uneven. Glad I did it...glad to get out of there.

Once back down at the base, we noticed the flow had entered a kipuka and that a tree had begun to vaporize. Trees sometimes just seem to turn into a cloud of steam and then explode, leaving nothing of the tree in the ground and sending wood shrapnel in all directions. The tree exploded. I asked Yvonne if she knew how to get over to that spot right away...it was a hundred yards away with ten-minute-old pillow lava between us and the ex-tree. Pillow lava is still semi-liquid and gives when you step on it, but may hold just long enough to let you get across it. She agreed to lead me across. I wanted to get over there quickly so I could, for the first time, photograph a fresh lava tree mold...the hollow spot where the tree had stood that would soon fill with lava, leaving no trace. I knew we had just a few minutes to get that shot.

CJ was already at the lava tree mold. The two Germans were with me. I told them to sit still until I got back. One agreed right away. The other, Karsten, wanted to go with me. I told Karsten that his shoes might melt off his feet and that he would be quite uncomfortable after that happened. He wanted to go anyway.

On the website, there is a link to the video that Karsten took of me scrambling across the pillow lava. It will be horrifying to anyone not used to being out on the lava. Toward the end of the 45-second video, the soles of his shoes catch fire and begin to melt. Had I not had duct tape with me, he might still be out there.

Lava hikes up the pali are for the young and foolish or for the just plain foolish. Glad I did it this time and would sure like to do a couple more, but not too many more.

The lava hike up to Pu'u'O'o

Pu'u'O'o is the other crater on Kilauea volcano. It is about eight miles from the main Halema'uma'u crater and has been the most active over the past decade or so. It is in an extremely remote location and it is surrounded by myths and stories that would discourage anyone with a brain from venturing anywhere near it. The closest most of us will ever come to it is by helicopter...and it is quite a sight.

I think it is illegal to venture out to Pu'u'O'o on foot. I know there is no approved access to it. I believe you would have to cross private property, going through a never-ending tropical rain forest with mud up to your waist and mosquitos large enough to abduct you, and only then would you emerge onto a lava field so hot, so gas-filled, so cracked and scary that only a fool would dare to venture out there. And about a dozen of us launched our Pu'u'O'o adventure.

I hiked out with Nick Selway and Sarah Buzzetti. We had two guides and about a half dozen other fools with us. I really had no idea what to expect. Good thing...had I known I would have never gone. It was a death march.

It took us hours to get through the forest. I had consumed much of my water and all of my power bars by the time we got out of the Never-Ending Forest. And when we emerged...there it was... Pu'u'O'o in all of its glory, pumping out lava like a son of a gun.

The edge of the forest was on fire. I had never really been that close to a lava-sparked forest fire and thought I might get some interesting photos. I ran ahead of the group toward the burning trees. About that time, one of the trees exploded, sending a giant limb directly over my head. I decided that I should have tried to get shots like that shot with my long lens...and I retreated.

One of the reasons not a lot of photographers venture out to Pu'u'O'o is that it is difficult to get a decent photograph out there. I know there are some classics by people like Bryan Lowry, but no one would be getting any great shots on the day I was there. The heat shimmer was everywhere...hell, the heat was everywhere.

It was quite a sight, but not great for photography. Glad I went, but happy to get out of there. Our timing on when to leave was determined for us when a passing shower turned the scene into a deadly whiteout and sent all of us running for the trail in the tree line.

The trip back was just plain horrible. I have run a dozen marathons, climbed mountains, lived through track and field workouts that made me puke. But this was on another level. I started off at the front of the pack. Within half an hour the only people behind me were the two 300-hundred pound fellow hikers whom I was surprised were even still alive and, happily, one of the guides. She finally came up to me and said, "Uncle (that is what we call old guys in Hawaii), would you like me to carry your pack?" Oh hell, yes...the pack is yours. I gave it to her and sprinted off before she could notice how heavy it was.

I caught up with the middle of the group and I guess I looked like death. One nice couple offered me a Gatorade, which I consumed without ever putting it down. Another offered me a power bar, which I think I removed the wrapper from before eating it in about three bites. My strength was restored and I took off determined to stay way ahead of the guide, just in case she changed her mind.

I got back to our cars probably twenty minutes before the 300-pounders and the guide. She brought over my pack and gave it to me. I handed her every penny I had on me...$85, and my thanks. She said, "Uncle, for $85 next time I will carry YOU both ways." My kind of woman.

So, the fifth kind of lava hike...the Pu'u'O'o hike...forget it.

CHAPTER NINE

You Meet the Strangest People on the Rim of the Volcano in the Middle of the Night

I live on an island with a very active volcano. That volcano produces amazing amounts of lava and fumes...huge toxic clouds that shoot straight up from the caldera. It is always fun to photograph, but the scene is particularly spectacular at night. It is best to photograph late at night in summer when the Milky Way rainbows directly over the caldera and on nights when there is no moon. Hawaii Volcanoes National Park is where I want to be on those special nights.

So, about ten o'clock at night, I turn to my photographer wife and say, "Hey, let's head out to the volcano and shoot all night." More often than not, she says "yes" and off we go. On this particular night, she said, "No...you go," and off I went.

It takes about an hour and a half to drive to the volcano from my house. The road is dark and curvy and one lane each way. It is a boring drive at night and the road can get you if you do not pay attention. I blasted some music and made good time. When I got there around midnight the volcano was blazing away under a cloudless Milky Way-filled sky and I was all alone. I had the park to myself.

I drove out to a remote location that affords a great view of the caldera with a cliff-hanging tree in the foreground. It is a bit of a walk to get there with just a flashlight illuminating the trail and the volcano glow lighting up the sky. That particular night it was cold and windy, 48 degrees at the 4500-foot level where I would be photographing, with 25-mile-per-hour winds. Cold as heck.

The tree is next to a cliff that drops down a couple hundred feet, so I am pretty careful as I set up my tripod and camera close to that tree and the cliff edge. I light up the tree with my flashlight to help me gain focus for my camera and notice a fresh offering to Madame Pele...the goddess of fire and volcanoes in the Hawaiian culture. It is a traditional offering of flowers and leaves, some alcohol and coins. It looked like it had just been placed there.

I am extremely respectful of those who keep the Hawaiian culture alive on this island. They connect the past to the present. I often run into Native Hawaiians conducting cultural practices out in the lava fields or near the volcano and I give them their space and privacy. As soon as I saw the offering, I decided I would take one photo from this location and move elsewhere, as I suspected there might be people I could not see in the dark who I had interrupted, and I did not want to interfere. I set up the tripod and camera, attached a cord release to the shutter and stepped back to take my shot.

As I extended my foot backwards, it landed on a foot...a human foot. I whirled around and my nose was resting directly in the middle of the chest of a HUGE guy. The guy had to be six-foot-six or taller. He had on a tee shirt, shorts and slippas (flip flops). The guy was haole (a white guy like me) and he stood there like a statue. I couldn't really talk. I just blabbered a few sentences...one after another. "I didn't hear you coming.... I'm sorry I stepped on you...didn't mean to.... You look cold. Can I get you a sweater from my car?"

No answer of any kind.

I kept apologizing and asking questions. Nothing. By now, the thought occurred to me that he might be ready to push me off the cliff. I kept talking and quietly grabbed the tripod in one hand. My plan...try to get in one good swing and, hopefully, hit him hard in the side of the head with my expensive camera. Still nothing from him. Finally I said, "Hey...I'm a Kona boy...west side. How 'bout you...Hilo boy...east side?" More nothing. I repeated the question and then he finally spoke. His answer...an angry finger pointing to the ground and the word, "Here." I said, "You mean Hilo?" He said, "No. Here."

I strengthened my grip on the tripod. I figured he was done with the conversation. I was right. He turned quickly, moved over to the edge of the cliff and swiftly walked away into the dark, finally completely disappearing in the distance...not magically disappearing....just disappearing into the dark. I grabbed my gear and got the hell out of there.

When I got to the parking lot, there was my car...no other cars...no bikes... nothing. I mention that because we were a long way from civilization...no one lives anywhere nearby. That big guy had needed some way to get out there. I got in my car and drove home...it was a long, dark, disturbing ride home.

When I got home, at maybe 3 a.m., I edited the one crappy photo I had taken... which included a photo of the sacrifice left for Madame Pele...and posted it on Facebook along with a paragraph-long story of the events of that evening. The next morning when I got up, three people had commented that exact same thing had happened to them at that same tree over the course of the past three years. The experience had left all of us shaken.

The next night, my partner Nick stayed out at a hotel near the volcano. He mentioned the story to our friend who runs the hotel. She stopped him at the beginning and told him the story...word for word. Even got the part right about looking the big guy right in the face and not being able to describe his features. Got it right about the "here" answer and his clothing and his huge size and his appearing out of nowhere...got it all right. Nick asked how she knew this story. She said, "Easy...I've heard that same story...word for word...from dozens of people over the last 40 years."

So...I still go out to that spot in the middle of the night. I tend to turn around frequently and sweep the area with my flashlight. I never feel particularly safe there. I would really prefer never to meet that guy again. But the volcano calls to me and draws me back and I will keep going. And the photos I get, I love. If you wanted to go along with me...I could use the company. Aloha.

P.S. I wrote this "incident report" before the caldera at Halema'uma'u collapsed during the Puna eruption of 2018. I no longer go out to the volcano at night. The access to it is closed. Much of the caldera collapsed and it does not look anything like it used to. As of this writing, there is no lava back in the bottom of the caldera, but an acidic lake is growing there. It was spooky enough before the collapse...no way I am going out there alone at the moment. But things change, and I am hoping to see it ablaze once again in the future. I'll take my chances then.

CHAPTER TEN

The Puna Eruption of 2018

The Puna District is on the other side of the island from where I live, some two hours away by car. It is the rainy, windward side of the island, the side that catches the brunt of any major storm that comes our way. It is lush, tropical, unique and beautiful. Because it is also very active volcanically, you can get a lot of land there for a small amount of money. Puna District is located in an area designated by the United States Geological Survey as Lava Zone 1 or 2...the most active lava zones on the island. In the years before the 2018 eruption, you could find hot spots, hot pools and steam vents in many places throughout the Puna area. The residents there knew the dangers.

In 2014 a lava flow from the Pu'u'O'o vent travelled all the way to Pahoa, a small town at the high end of the Puna District. The flow stopped literally at the fence line to the city. A bullet dodged.

In 2018, the phones lit all over the Big Island. There was a huge earthquake...a 6.9, and hundreds of other smaller quakes. At one point, all of the lava in the Halema'umu'a crater disappeared. Uh oh. Shortly there-after, all the lava in the Pu'u'O'o crater disappeared. Double uh oh. Wait for it. All of a sudden, earthquakes and cracks and fissures filled with lava opened up in the Leilani Estates subdivision and the eruption was on.

Those who lived on this island in the 1950s and beyond have seen this kind of eruption several times. It was all new to me. By the time I got over to Leilani Estates to help evacuate a friend, things were trending toward full-on disaster. Leilani Estates and several other beautiful communities in that area were squarely in the middle of the eruption.

What does a volcanic eruption look like when it's in the middle of a community? It is one of the saddest and scariest things I have ever witnessed. That area was experiencing a thousand earthquakes a day, with at least one of them being 5.0 or higher. The ground was always moving as the lava ran in lava tubes beneath it.

Everywhere you looked, there were cracks in the ground and in the structures. The place was being torn apart. Most of the cracks had large clouds of steam and gas pouring out of them. Others had lava oozing out. We saw a house completely covered with a coating of sulfur. Other cracks built into splatter cones with lava fireworking out of their tops. And then there were the fissures...huge holes in the ground out of which came great volumes of lava. The biggest one of those was fissure #8 right in the middle of Leilani Estates. At its height, it was shooting lava 200 feet or more into the air 24/7 for weeks on end.

Fissure #8 created a river of lava that in places was 400 yards across and seven or eight miles long...it reached to the sea. That lava flow covered that treasure of a community, Kapoho, and the world-class tidal ponds that existed there. The lava filled in the hot pool that so many of us used and loved near Pohoiki. And at Pohoiki, the lava flow almost reached the "harbor" and launch ramp used by my buddy Shane for his lava excursions and then filled in that area with black sand, cutting off the ramp from the sea. In Kapoho, the lava pushed the shoreline another half mile or more out to sea, covering hundreds of homes as it moved forward.

The river also filled in the state of Hawaii's biggest freshwater lake, Green Lake. It had been some 400 feet deep and the lava evaporated it in about a day. Once the lake was filled up, a bit of lava spilled over briefly onto a low area beside the lake, creating a brief 40-foot tall lava waterfall. I was fortunate to photograph that in good conditions from 3000 feet above in a helicopter...the clearest shot of it anyone took, and one shared across the internet and on the news.

I will leave the full description of the eruption to those who actually know the facts, like the geologists, the residents of that area and the historians. This was a well-documented eruption and you can find out whatever you want to know by searching "2018 lower Puna eruption" on the internet.

But I want to share a couple of stories that you will not find on the internet...

CHAPTER ELEVEN

Turd Drops Three Stories Into Circle of Friends

Our buddy Shane had a house in lower Puna and a boat shed where he kept and serviced his boats. Both were in harm's way during the eruption. In fact, the lava was flowing just past the tree line on his property and we all expected that the buildings would go at any moment. So, a bunch of us got together and put in a lot of effort to save what we could save.

By the way...the world was run by rumors during the chaos of the eruption. One of those rumors had to do with the Puna Geothermal Venture nearby...like easy-walking-distance nearby. That lab somehow produced electricity from the magma at the bottom of wells below the surface. The rumor was that they used a chemical in the process that, when the lava hit it and caused it to explode, would kill everyone around. So, there was that to worry about.

The boat shed had a house attached to it. The shed part was about two stories high and the house was taller. On the walls of the shed were several of Shane's 500-horsepower engines for his lava boats. If you had been out on the water with us you would know why he needed extra engines...those engines worked in a tough environment. So Shane kept spares around and my guess is they were expensive... very expensive. They needed to be evacuated.

Not only were the engines expensive, we felt that the racks they were on were also quite valuable. So those who actually knew something about how to build and take things apart decided to stop work for a moment and discuss our next steps (trust me, I had no clue and was basically an observer to this part of the work). We were worried about the approaching lava and how long we might have before we had to evacuate, so the group asked one of the more agile guys to go up to the top story, crawl out the window onto the roof and work his way up to the peak of the roof to get a clear view of the lava flow and its proximity. Off he went.

The group had done some preliminary work to extricate the engines and racks from the wall. They cut some PVC pipes that were in the way and pulled out some electrical wiring. But it was still going to be a difficult thing to do safely and it needed everyone's input.

Our agile guy got up to the peak of the roof and saw what he needed to see. It was his opinion that we did not have much time left. So, on the way down, he stopped in the bathroom to take the only civilized dump he was going to get to take that day. He took care of his business and came back downstairs to give us his report.

What our agile guy did not know was that one of the PVC pipes we had already cut was the pipe directly from the upstairs toilet to the septic tank. So, when he flushed the toilet, what was in that toilet rushed down the stub of the PVC pipe until it hit open air and from there dropped directly into the middle of the circle of friends trying to engineer the rack and engine removals. Splash!

I can tell you accurately that such an event will cause a half dozen people to all jump backwards in unison. After that, we all crept in to see what had landed in our midst...and then we looked up. I can still hear the laughter.

Agile guy joins us shortly thereafter. He is smiling, but not for long. Hard to live that one down.

I was one of several old guys on the team trying to save stuff from Shane's house and boat shed. I was also the least useful. Much of this was heavy lifting stuff and my old body is just not up to much of that. So, to be of some use, I was going around the property trying to find the things of the highest possible value and kind of triaging the evacuation. One of the things I found was a large box with a sign on it that read, "For the Egyptian Museum in Cairo." What the heck would Shane have for that wonderful museum? Whatever it was, it had to be valuable. So, I opened the box. Out flew two live chickens, right into my face. I almost did my own version of Agile Guy, damn near shitting my pants. The rest of the team loved it. They had set me up.

At night it was spooky as heck out there. There was no electricity, so it was dark except for the ubiquitous red glow from the lava. Anyone who was there will never forget the sounds, lava explosions, steam and gas explosions, propane tank explosions. The sound of lava exiting a fissure at high speed was like the sound of a Roman Candle firing. When you heard it, you instinctively looked up.

We could not work safely at night and anyway we had to rest at some point, so work came to a halt. The area was under TIGHT control by the authorities who were concerned both for the safety of their people and for that of people who were still not evacuated...and everyone had very real concerns about the looting that was going on. It was like a war zone.

With that as background, and knowing full well that I am a photographer and this is a once in a lifetime opportunity, you may not be surprised that I snuck off the premises to take a few photos. I didn't take a lot because I got the daylights scared out of me right away when I was enveloped in a gas cloud that offered no actual oxygen for my professional gas mask to filter. But what I did get from the ground were shots I am likely never going to be able to match. It was a spectacular look into the third ring of Hell.

I had noticed technology around that I suspected was some kind of video feed, probably used by the authorities to keep track of the lava flow and anyone wandering around out there. Unfortunately, I noticed those just after I saw a little red light go off. That spooked me. Should have. Two minutes later a police car comes barreling down that road. I saw it coming and jumped in the cane grass to hide. The police officer stopped absolutely in front of where I jumped into the grass. He pulled out a flashlight that looked like a beacon and started sweeping it over the area and yelling excitedly that he saw me go in there and wasn't leaving until I surrendered. I did not move. He then yelled that he was sending his dog in after me. Again I did not move—I was sure he had no dog and I was right. "Fuck you, copper, you will never take me alive," I said in my head. What I really said was nothing, I just sat there silent and scared to death. He looked for maybe three minutes, told me he would be waiting up the street to catch me when I came out and then said—and I will never forget this line—"Have a nice day."

Well, it was not "day." It was the middle of the night. I was trying to keep from choking from the volcanic gas. I could hear the lava popping not all that far away and I was still hiding in the cane grass, along with a bunch of centipedes, I guessed...so, no, it was unlikely that I was going to "have a nice day."

I waited about a half hour to come out. That gave me plenty of time to contemplate how it was that a nice retired CEO and charitable foundation president was now hiding out from the police in the cane grass to keep from a possible felony arrest. When I did emerge, I worked my way around where I knew that camera was set up, made it into a tree line and tacked my way back to Shane's place. That was the last of my nighttime adventures in the lava zone.

I had my own Agile Guy moment when I decided that I could no longer stand my own smell and went in to take a shower. I got naked and soaped up so I could conserve whatever water was still available. I then turned on the shower. There was no water. That was an odd moment.

I could tell you about trying to catch a peacock to get him to safety. Here is a hint...don't try to catch a peacock.

Shane and his makeshift crew managed to save many of his possessions, including several engines and tools. However, he lost much to the lava. We pulled out what we could, but the lava waits for no one.

In the end, we all left together. Tears were shed. Prayers were said and we all headed in different directions.

I headed to the Hilo airport. I had an opportunity to be over the lava flow in the front seat of a doors-off helicopter on several occasions during the eruption. Each time it was a mind-blowing experience. Seeing a seven- or eight-mile-long river of lava paving over communities and filling in beautiful beaches was one of the saddest and most beautiful things I have ever seen. By pure coincidence, I photographed a flower farm just as it was taken by the lava...it was owned by a friend of mine from long ago on the mainland. He called me just as we landed back in Hilo and told me he was at the Kona International Airport on his way back to California. I told him I had just photographed his farm and he asked me to send him the photos so he could have some closure. I did.

Linda and I also went up in a small plane on the last night of the eruption. We went up with CJ at sunset and caught the last gasp of Fissure #8. The highlight of that trip was the fact that I had not closed my door correctly and it came open as I leaned against it during a steep turn over the fissure. That was a thrill. Thankfully, I was triple-belted in and we were able to get the door closed. I wonder if I would have kept firing my camera all the way down the 3000-foot drop to the ground had I actually fallen out? No one will ever know.

Hey...one happy story in all of this. Linda and I were working the gallery one night. We close at 9:30 p.m. At 9:20 a nice family from California came in and struck up a conversation. I asked them how long they would be on island and they said they were leaving the next day. I asked if they got to do everything they wanted. They said yes, except they had not gotten to see the Milky Way. I told them that my wife was in the back, that I had a truck full of warm clothes and cameras and tripods and snacks and that Linda and I were heading up Mauna Kea volcano in just ten minutes to photograph the Milky Way on a moonless night. I told them we would be at about 8000 feet and it should be clear and that we would show them how to properly photograph the beautiful night sky, all for the low, low price of zero. They quickly agreed to join us.

What I did not know was that not only was the Milky Way in the absolutely perfect position to photograph, but that lower Puna was lit up like sunrise by the eruption, some forty or so miles away. As we got out of our cars, I asked them to wait for a few minutes so I could get what I thought might be the photo of a lifetime for me. I got that photo and it is one that makes me proud to be a photographer. Linda got great shots as well and then we made sure that each member of their family got their shot of a lifetime. I still hear from them. Turned out to be a great night for all of us.

When the Puna eruption was all done, I was all done, mentally and physically. It had worn me out, long days and nights of work and photography, filling in at the gallery for CJ who spent ten times more hours at the eruption than I did. The air in Kona was just plain disgusting, filled with volcanic particles that would pile up on window sills and were doing our lungs no good either. No one was traveling to the island because they could not get anywhere near the eruption or into the National Park. Business was slow. Friends were losing their homes, their health and their livelihoods. I was having bad dreams about the eruption and not getting much sleep. Bad times indeed. I was thankful when it stopped.

And as soon as it was over, Linda and I headed to Tanzania and Kenya to put the last few months out of our heads. Best move ever. A "sorbet" moment in our lives that we both sorely needed.

CHAPTER TWELVE

Escape to Africa for the Trip of a Lifetime

My wife and I are seasoned (that means about 70 years of age) professional adventure photographers who have visited over 100 countries. We're spoiled rotten when it comes to travel. We like unique travel and we seek opportunities to see things few people see, with an expert or two alongside for guidance. We want to feel safe and comfortable in our travels and we want to be well taken care of along the way.

Up until recently, the biggest thing left undone on our list of things we wanted to experience was an African safari. We knocked that one off the list at the end of 2018, with the impressive help of Thomson Safaris. I will leave it to them to explain the services they provide, but they were just plain perfect for what we wanted to do.

Our trip took us to Tanzania for 11 days in Tarangire National Park and the Serengeti along the Mara River. I had never seen so much wildlife in a natural setting—huge numbers and great diversity of birds, big animals, monkeys, reptiles—and the oddest trees I have ever seen.

We were in vehicles that were built for off-road conditions and perfect for photographers or anyone wanting to see things up close and personal. Alongside us was Craig Sholley of the African Wildlife Foundation and various experienced local guides—all there to make sure we saw what there was to see, understood what we were seeing and stayed safe in the process.

During our time in the bush, we went out twice a day on safari. Every single time we went out, we scored something surprising and interesting. One morning we found a family of lions within ten minutes of our camp. Another morning we encountered a cheetah chasing a hartebeest, and then the herd of hartebeests turned on the cheetah and nearly ran him down right in front of us. We saw a leopard bound up a tree like it was on flat land, an elephant shake a tree so hard the nuts in the tree fell to the ground for him to eat. We also saw two lions kill and eat a warthog, which is hard to imagine because a warthog is a very tough and dangerous-looking animal. Giraffes walked right by our vehicle and looked inside to see if we were friend or foe. One afternoon we came across a water hole with hundreds of resting hippos.

We never had an uneventful excursion; they were all off the charts.

As a kid, I watched adventure travel shows on TV and elsewhere, and they created a couple of imagined pictures that I have carried in my head for decades, shots I wanted to get during my lifetime. There were two in particular.

One was of the Mara River Great Migration Crossing, where thousands of wildebeests, zebras and other animals dive off a riverside cliff into a croc-infested river to try to make it to the other side where they can find food and water for part of the year. The other shot I had imagined was of elephants walking in the trees with an orange African sunset directly in front of them. Happy to say, I scored both on this trip.

Even though we timed the trip to maximize our chances of seeing a Mara River crossing, there was no guarantee that it would happen as planned. So one morning we headed out from camp and noticed tens of thousands of animals all heading for the river in lines that stretched for miles. We headed for the river ourselves and found thousands more all grouped at the river's edge. All that was needed was for one of them to take a leap and show the others the way. Our guide hid our vehicle behind a bush, shut off the engine and the wait began. We did not have to wait long.

Within a couple of minutes, we could hear a commotion and see vast clouds of dust rise up in the air. The herd was on the move. Our driver rushed us up to the cliff, and we could not believe our eyes—it was complete chaos. Wildebeests stampeded behind the vehicle, in front of the vehicle, ten feet below us on a ledge and on a cliffside just a few hundred feet in front of us. Within moments, we were positioned so we could see them leaping from the cliff to the river and landing on the water, each other and the rocks. The noise was intense. We could feel their panic. They seemed to fully understand they could be swept away or wedged between rocks or grabbed by a HUGE croc. Thousands of animals crossed in three big columns over the next forty minutes.

When the lucky ones reached the other side (and happy to say, there were few casualties during this crossing) there was more chaos. The other side was steep and slippery and crowded beyond belief with wildebeests and zebras. Watching them claw their way up the cliffside opposite us was just amazing.

And then it stopped. It came to an absolute halt, not a single animal in the water. That was it for the day. Next to me was my wife and next to her was one of the world's great wildlife and landscape photographers, Jeff Vanuga.

Jeff said to me, "What did you think of that crossing?" I said, "I can't talk," and I couldn't; I was completely choked up with emotion. This had been one of the great moments of my life.

I had captured the image I had imagined decades ago and had been carrying in my head ever since, exactly as I had imagined it.

The image featured a wildebeest jumping off a cliff through a beam of light that illuminated only that single animal. Here's how it happened. Once I got over my initial frenzy of shots when we first arrived at the cliff, I took a moment to look for a beam of light and found it. I set my telephoto on that beam and waited for a wildebeest to leap directly through it, and one did immediately. I could not believe my luck.

Another evening, Jeff, my wife and I rolled up on a herd of elephants in some trees with the sun setting in front of them, an orange African sun. We all knew what we had stumbled upon, the perfect "elephants at sunset in the tree line" scene and we immediately started taking photos. Scored again.

Our trip did have a few oddities along the way. The first involved a chemical toilet in our tent.

We camped out in luxury—big beautiful tents, a warm shower each night and a chemical toilet. Good thing, because if you went out at night you would probably be eaten by something large. I am not kidding. Linda was escorted back to our tent one night by a guard and she asked if she really needed the protection. He turned his light toward the bush that surrounded us and thirty sets of eyes beamed back. Later that night, a lion took down a zebra and actually bumped against our tent in the process. That was the end of that sleep cycle for us. In the morning, the lion was drinking out of a bucket of water not twenty feet from out tent, face covered in blood. We decided to wait a while before going to breakfast.

One half day on the safari, I fell ill. Got the trots. No fun. Linda went off on the afternoon excursion and I stayed at home to recover. That night, one of the guides came to see if I could eat anything. I thought I could and asked for some bread—they made excellent bread. He brought us garlic bread, which we did not notice until late at night.

By now it was time to go to sleep. I think everyone else in camp was already asleep. It was then we realized that I had not eaten the garlic bread. We had been strongly and repeatedly warned against having any food in our tents...not even in wrappers. Animals would claw through the canvas tents and come inside to find the food. What to do?

I came up with a great idea. Let's toss the garlic bread into the chemical toilets. That ought to drown out the food smell...right? Into the toilets it went. Problem solved...until morning.

When we opened the toilet lid to use it in the morning, we were both forced out of the bathroom by the stench. It was life-altering. We decided quickly that we would not need to go to the bathroom that day. Instead, we dressed for breakfast and left. We begged one of the staff to get us a new toilet. He said they would clean it for us. I told him that was not good enough...we needed a new one. I produced $50 American. We had a new toilet by the time breakfast was finished. Lesson learned.

The second little story had to do with a small plane trip we took from a dirt runway in one part of Tanzania to another. I quickly figured out that the only decent seat for photography was the vacant co-pilot seat. I knew from the map that we would be flying over an active volcano, a lake and the Ngorongoro Crater, all of which I wanted to photograph. So I approached the pilot and let him know that I had nearly a thousand hours in that particular aircraft. He invited me to sit next to him up front.

About fifteen minutes into the flight, he offered me the opportunity to take command and fly the plane. I told him I had no idea how to fly the plane. He said, "You told me you had a thousand hours in this plane." I said I did...as a passenger. The rest of the flight was flown in silence. I got some nice shots.

And at the start of our trip we had this magical encounter...

The road from Kilimanjaro International Airport toward Tarangire National Park is a long, straight, two-lane paved highway. The road can be congested in the daytime with cars, small motorcycles, pedestrians, vendors, animal-drawn carts and small herds of animals tended by one or two Maasai. Along the road in most places, there are either bare-bones retail shops or vacant land with dust everywhere. When we did encounter people in larger groups, they tended to be colorfully dressed and fully animated, except the shop keepers who seemed to be mostly women sitting in front of the stores, looking dejected and bored while waiting for a customer. Open-air food vendors were everywhere...cooking corn or other staples on barbecue setups of all kinds. Young men sitting on small motorcycles are omnipresent, waiting for what...I do not know. Miles down that road, our off-road vehicle would turn abruptly onto a fairly rough dirt road and a few miles later we were at the entrance of Tarangire National Park...a huge park that is completely devoid of any development and filled with all the creatures that nature placed there...lions, elephants, leopards, giraffes, monkeys, gazelle and on and on...a first-class safari land for adventure photographers or anyone else who wants to see what nature looks like up close.

Midway along the road from Arusha, one of our party had to "check a tire," code for "take a leak." Our driver pulled over, looked around to see if the area looked safe from animals (we were now well out into the countryside or "the middle of nowhere," as I would normally call it) and pointed toward a bush. Our friend headed toward cover and we waited patiently...for about ten seconds.

Out of nowhere, there was a knock on my car window. Caught me by surprise, as I had seen no one there when we pulled up. (My wife tells me she believes a car pulled up and four people got out when I was not looking). I noticed movement to my left...two men heading directly toward our lady in the bushes. I started to jump out of the car on the left side to intervene, but the two men veered off in another direction. I then turned back to see who was knocking on my window. It was a tall, beautiful, young black lady. I pushed open my window and she said to me, in perfect English, "This is my son and he has always wanted to meet you." I looked down, and there was her three-year-old, good-looking, smiling son looking up at me. She then said that he wanted to shake my hand. There was no door on that side of the vehicle and I was a bit confused as to what was really going on, so I just leaned way out the window and shook the young man's hand. He got a huge grin on his face and got emotional. He said something to his mom that I could not understand. As he looked back at me, she said, "This is a bit embarrassing, but he would like to kiss you." I leaned out again...even further this time...picked him up under his arms and raised him up to my level...and I then planted a big kiss on his forehead.

Once again on the ground, the young man stepped back, smiled that big smile of his and gave me a double shaka. A shaka is a Hawaiian hand gesture that is kind of like a "thumbs up" in meaning....thumb pointed out, little finger pointed out... middle three fingers pulled into your palm and then the whole hand is shaken back and forth...a very friendly greeting in Hawaii. It kind of startled me, as it was the last gesture I expected to see in Africa. At that, the young lady thanked me, said I made her son very happy and wished me well. They moved off with the young man continuing to look back and wave at me.

There were four of us in the car and we all witnessed this event. We all went silent, as the tire checker got back in the car and we prepared to drive off. Later I asked the driver if he had witnessed what had happened. He had and said he spoke briefly with her when they first showed up. He asked her if she was Maasai, as we were in the heart of Maasai territory and she did not look, or dress, like a Maasai. She said she was not, that she had married a Maasai. The driver said this was extremely unusual. Women from outside the Maasai community do not normally voluntarily sign up for the role a woman plays in Maasai life because it can be difficult. But she had done so happily and lived nearby.

The driver knew nothing else about her. I asked him if he had heard what she said to me. He smiled and said he had. I asked him what he thought of that. He told me that what I heard and what she probably meant were likely two different things. I asked him what he thought she meant. He said, "My son has always wanted to meet an old white guy." There was a moment of silence and then all of us in the car started laughing.

He was probably right, but that is not what she said and it makes a better dream story in my head and in this writing if she had said exactly what she meant.

I asked him about the shaka. He said it was not a hand gesture used in that part of the world and he had never seen it used by a Maasai or anyone other than a few Hawaiian visitors such as ourselves. He too thought the whole encounter was dream-like and highly unusual.

One last thing...as I put the young man back down on the ground after kissing him, I noticed a medical port in the back of his hand...the kind used to deliver intravenous drugs. That gave me pause for thought. My first thought was concern for the young man...I wondered what serious illness he was fighting (I have to say that he looked like he was winning that battle, whatever it was). My second thought was, "What have I just exposed myself to?" Happy to say it has been over a year since that encounter and I am still healthy but still a bit confused by the whole episode with the lady and her son.

I wish I had not been so startled and had taken a few photos of her and her son and asked for their names. They asked me for nothing other than the interaction. They could not have been nicer. I would love to know their whole story but I never will.

And so, for the entire safari...in between photo ops...I ran the story over and over in my head until it has now developed into a book length tale that I may or may not write. If I do, 99 percent of it will be fictional. The one percent that will be factual will be the words written here...all real and all a mystery. My welcome to Tanzania...half a world away from my home in Hawaii...is one that I will never forget.

CHAPTER THIRTEEN

In the Water and Face-To-Face With a
15-Foot-Long Salt Water Crocodile

I have run into salt water and similar crocodiles in Australia, Panama, Egypt, Central America and Tanzania. On none of those occasions did it occur to me that it would be a good idea to hop into the water with them and take their photo. Then in 2015, all of a sudden, it did seem like a good idea...and I did it.

I have a friend named Eli Martinez. Eli owns *Shark Diver Magazine,* has hosted shows during the Discovery Channel's *Shark Week* and leads excursions all around the world to do seemingly idiotic things, like swimming with orcas in the dead of winter off Norway, photographing the world's biggest anacondas in their native habitat (underwater in a river in Brazil), hand-feeding huge tiger sharks in the Bahamas and...yes...getting in the water with 15-foot long, 2000-pound salt water crocodiles in a remote part of Mexico. The spot with the crocs...about 40 miles offshore from the extremely small and remote Mexico/Belize border "town" of Xcalak, Mexico, at a Mexican national wildlife preserve called Banco Chinchorro.

Eli asked me to join him for the croc adventure. My wife and I had already done several adventures with Eli involving whale sharks and assorted other ocean creatures. We trust Eli...up to a point. I say up to a point because his idea of danger and mine are in two different ledgers. He is very comfortable doing crazy things that I would never think of doing on my own.

So, I did my research. I think that Eli sensed, just like my buddies CJ and Nick in other circumstances, that if I knew the whole truth I would not be going on this adventure. So Eli gave me his version of the truth. He told me that the crocs would be well-fed and lazy before we ever got in the water. We would be swimming when the sun was hot and the crocs were resting. We would be well-protected. Said we would hop over to the islands where the crocs live in a fast boat. Told me the accommodations out there were rustic and basic, but adequate. Should be fun.

I asked him if there was any danger that one of the crocs could get inside the protective cage and grab us. He assured me there was no such danger. I found out later that he was 100-percent truthful on that piece...there was no protective cage!

I signed up. Linda caught a glimpse of the "rustic and basic accommodations" and opted out. She said she would meet me the next week for a whale shark adventure with Eli off of Isla Mujeres, Mexico. I went on my own to Cancun and met up with Eli. We headed south to Xcalak, as far south as you can go in that part of Mexico without leaving the country, nearly six hours by van from Cancun.

The accommodations in Xcalak WERE rustic and basic. It was a cinder block dive center located on the beach featuring a few rooms and a bar/café. We stayed overnight and explored the area. The next day, we boarded long, narrow modern boats with two powerful engines, picked our way through the reef to open water and put the pedal to the metal for the two hour-plus trip across open ocean to Banco Chinchorro. This was hurricane season, and I had already barely survived one tropical storm in Mexico with Eli, so I was wary of the passage and happy to arrive on the atoll reef.

Once there, we found that our accommodations were neither rustic nor basic, but they were adequate, consisting of a fisherman's shelter up on stilts in a lagoon just off a very small island in the marine reserve. The island was home to over a hundred large salt water crocodiles and a few nervous birds. Other than the various fishermen's shacks in the area, there was nothing...truly the middle of nowhere.

There were ten of us on this expedition....six guests, Eli, the boat driver and his assistant, and a croc expert/safety guy from Xcalak. The fisherman's shelter was in a lagoon with clear water that was four to six feet deep. There was a small island a hundred yards away in one direction and a deeper ocean drop-off in the other direction. The water surrounding the preserve was about 80 feet deep. The shelter had hammocks and a convenient orange Lowe's bucket for a toilet. There was no electricity, no phone, no internet service, no potable water other than what we had brought with us, no fire, no refrigeration. Basic. In our group: two women, a young man of 12, my new buddy from London...Chris, who became my dive partner, Eli and his crew, one other gentleman from Germany, and Mathias, our 140-pound safety guy who turned out to be absolutely excellent at his job. Mathias was in charge of our only piece of safety gear...a wooden stick.

First morning on site, we got up and headed out to the deeper reefs to catch breakfast and some lion fish, which would be used to distract the crocs should they get too focused on any of us in the water. Turns out the crocs love lion fish despite their poisonous spines.

I don't dive...I snorkel. However, I wanted to be part of the breakfast roundup and sure as hell did not want to be left alone on the shelter on stilts while the everyone else went off to see part of a reef system I might otherwise never see. So they took me along and let me snorkel in about 80 feet of water while they gathered breakfast. I never mentioned this to Eli, but once they dumped everyone in the ocean and the divers sank to the bottom, the boat just left me and took off. I was now completely alone with only my camera for protection, forty miles off the shore of a remote part of Mexico in an area I believed was well-known for its bull shark population, with nothing in sight but ocean in any direction I looked. Below me were seven divers spearing fish. I tried to see if I could get their attention. I found out quickly that divers look around, but never look up. I did my best to stay on top of them as they moved along. I also about wore out my neck from looking around me every three seconds to see what impending doom was headed my way. I figured the boat drivers knew where the divers were going and would eventually pick them up at that spot, so I did not want to lose contact with them. My tactic worked, and we all got picked up in due course.

The divers had speared more than forty of the invasive poisonous lion fish, which we used later with the crocs, but also used for breakfast...our breakfast. We ate them raw after soaking them in chili and lemon juice, silently praying that the boat captain/cook had fileted away the poisonous parts. He had and they were delicious.

After breakfast the crew tossed a few fish scraps into the water and soon we could see a salt water croc slowly swimming out from the island. Eli pointed to me and told me to gear up. I was the oldest and so got first shot at being in the water with the croc. Lucky me.

Eli told me to put on twenty-five pounds of lead weight so I would stay anchored to the sand and not float. I asked why. He told me, "If you float, you die." I put on the weights. I noticed that my hands, normally steady as can be, were absolutely trembling. I held them up to Eli and said, "I think I'm scared." Eli looked at me and said, "I'm scared too, buddy." It was quiet after that.

Just for the record, it was not the middle, hottest part of the day when we first got in. It was still fairly early morning. The crocs had not been fed in any way and the one croc that was coming toward us looked hungry to me. They were in no sense lethargic or lazy. They were looking for food.

I was pretty cautious that first session in the water. I never touched the crocs with my camera housing or hand. I never got within three feet. I was happy to get out and happy to have done this thing without getting killed. I wanted to go home right then, but we had were several more days to go.

In the next few days I teamed up with my buddy, Chris Knight from London. Chris is a stud. He is a fireman. A movie actor in such films as the Harry Potter and Fast and Furious series, and he won the TV program *Fear Factor UK*. Chris is big, good-looking and fearless. I was happy to have him as my partner. I would pretty much hide behind him as we engaged the crocs...one to three of them at a time... urging him to get closer so I could get a great shot over his shoulder.

Over time I learned to get more comfortable with the crocs and got close enough to push against them with my camera housing, the reptiles' teeth right up against my camera housing dome. I would push their tails away from me with my hand as they turned to swim away. I observed that they always snapped UP.... and figured out that a foolish person could actually touch them under their lower jaw to trigger a snap that might make for a great close-up photo. Those "snaps" sounded like cannon fire. I also noticed that they were really good at figuring out who the weakest person in the water was and then they stayed focused on that person. Most often that person was me. I learned to never, ever take my eyes off of them. It was a staring contest.

We had several uncomfortable interactions with the crocs. They usually occurred when one croc decided to bolt off in response to another croc entering the area.

We had two close calls that really shook me up. The first one was an agitated croc that had forced me back onto the boat. Eli and Chris stayed in the water with the croc even when it joined them in "their" territory...the sand. The unwritten rule was that the sand was ours and the one-foot-higher grassy area was the crocs', but the crocs would occasionally violate that "rule." When they did come down onto the sand flat, they might become agitated and energized and start hopping up and down on their back legs with their mouths wide open. Or, much worse, they would flail their huge tails and turn the clear water into a curtain of sand inside of which they were looking for food and we (the food) could see nothing. Chris got caught in one of those sand storms. I watched helplessly from the boat as the croc we called Toothy charged Chris in that murky water and went right between his legs, exiting the other side with no trophies from Chris's anatomy. I think that was on our last day and I doubt that I got in the water after that event.

The second scare came on the boat. Eli and I were excitedly recapping the day. I had a camera in my hand and Eli had a beer in his. A croc launched six feet out of the water right next to the boat...I guess he wanted in on our conversation. It happened in a nanosecond. Eli's first reaction was to ask me if I had gotten the photograph. I had not. In fact, I now needed to use the Lowe's bucket.

We made it back to Xcalak racing a tropical storm, a rough ride as we hunkered down under a tarp quietly praying the whole way. I got a beautiful shot of the storm swirling above the end of the pier once we got to shore. I was so happy to be back on shore I thought seriously about kissing the ground. The photos I got from that trip have been in newspapers and on TV all around the world. We sell a few of the more startling ones in our gallery. It is amazing what you can do when you put your good sense and fears aside. Thankful to Eli for having me along on one of the great adventures of my life. I will put up a bunch of the photos on my website and you will not believe them.

CHAPTER FOURTEEN

An Open Ocean Swim With Hundreds of Whale Sharks

Whale sharks are huge. The ones we have encountered have been anywhere from 25 to 60 feet long. Their tails span twelve feet. Their skin is four inches thick. Their mouths are up to five feet across. These are massive, gentle, plankton-eating sea creatures. They are not a danger to humans. They are often hard to find...I never saw one until I was over sixty years of age.

My buddy in Kona, Joshua Lambus, is a fantastic ocean photographer. He got one of the first shots ever of a cookiecutter shark in its natural environment at night in the deep ocean off Kona. He was anxious to show me that photo, which appeared in *Shark Diver Magazine*. As he flipped through the pages to find it, he flipped past a photo that stopped me in my tracks....it was a photo from above of dozens of whale sharks. To hell with his cookiecutter shark, where was that photo taken?

It turns out that photo was taken off of Isla Holbox near the top of the thumb of the Yucatan Peninsula in Mexico. *Shark Diver Magazine* was organizing an excursion to go jump in the water with those giants. Count me in.

So, come July 2010, Linda, her best friend, Karin, and I headed to Mexico. I thought I was a hot-shot photographer. Linda was brand new to photography. But we had all the right gear and we were ready for an adventure.

First, the long drive across the Yucatan in a van. Eli warned us we would be held up at one point and he was right. A truck load of bad guys pulled out of the brush and stopped us. Eli got out and negotiated with them and I think we all tossed in $20 USD to pay the "toll." Once we got to the other side of the Yucatan, we took a ferry boat for an hour to the small island of Isla Holbox. Isla Holbox is beautiful, peaceful, dirt streets, golf carts for cars and enough mosquitos for one and all to enjoy. From Holbox we would launch out to sea each day to try to find the whale sharks.

I had a brand new water housing for my brand new Canon 5D Mark II camera. I had never actually put the camera into the housing, so I thought I would try that before we launched the next morning. I promptly dropped my new camera about four feet onto the tile floor. I had no back-up camera.

After quite a bit of work, I got the camera to function on one setting only.... ISO 100 (that was good...real good), f/4.5 (not horrible) and 1/100th of a second... way too slow for the action in the ocean. However, it was what it was...and I would have to make it work. Happy to say, I got several shots on that trip that we still sell to this day. Lucky as heck to get anything.

This whale shark adventure was a true adventure. Here's how it went...

We launched in search of the whale sharks in two boats each day. The boats were fast and each carried six or eight people. We cruised at high speed along the coastline toward Isla Contoy, quite a long ride. On the way, we saw a giant splash in the water and Eli stopped the boat and yelled for me to get in the water with my camera. Two things...I think Eli had somehow gotten the wrong impression that I really knew what I was doing...I mean, I had the good equipment and all and had been patting myself on the back from the moment I first met him, telling him what a great photographer I was, and I guess he believed me. Truth is...I did not know shit. Second, what in the hell was splashing around out there? Whatever it was... it had to be big....and now I was supposed to use all of my non-existent skills and knowledge to get close and photograph it? Third, I could barely get on my new, state-of-the-art, high-speed, professional swim fins. But...ego is ego, and I launched.

Turned out to be two of the biggest turtles I have ever seen locked in love's embrace trying their best to get away from me without disconnecting. Happy to say, I got some great shots and then swam back to the boat. When I got back I complained that the new fins had torn my feet to shreds...actually cut them up.... not good on the first day of a several-day ocean adventure. Eli reached over and removed the plastic shoe trees that were in the space where I had shoved my bare feet, the ones that should have been removed BEFORE the feet were crammed in there. It was at that point that Eli realized that I was a bit of a fraud and he would need to keep an eye on me.

When we got to Isla Contoy, we came upon a reef that was blocking our way to the grounds where we might find the whale sharks. Both boats came to rest and we surveyed the situation. The other boat turned around and headed to another, safer area for whale sharks. Eli and the captain talked their way through a game plan for getting through the pass without capsizing. They picked our line and laid the hammer down and made it through the pass in good order.

By now, we had been at sea a long time, hours. No whale sharks. It is a big ocean out there and you either find them or you do not. Just then, the radio lit up with news from other boats in the area. Our captain pointed us in a new direction and took off fast. Before long I looked out on an area the size of several football fields filled with the biggest shark fins I had ever seen. We had hit the mother lode.

The rest of the day was filled with whale shark encounters, manta ray encounters, mobius ray encounters, golden ray encounters and jellyfish and florescent egg colonies of all kinds. One of my best days in the ocean ever.

On the long way home, Eli collected all of our extra drinks and food and had the captain pull into a fish camp he had spotted on the way out. There were very young children running around without supervision of any kind, as their parents were out trying to catch lobsters to sell later. Eli pulled in, spoke to the children and gave them our supplies. They were joyous at the feast. For the next several days, we repeated this stop and by now most of us were saving as much food and drink as we could to give them. On our last day's stop, Dad and Mom were there to greet us and to give us some of the best lobsters you have ever seen as a thank you.

Speaking of lobsters....I am a picky eater. Holbox did not have much in the way of restaurants. However, Linda, Karin and I found a bar that had the best lobster pizza I will ever taste. There must have been two complete servings of lobster meat on each cheese pizza and the bar served bottled cold Coke to go with it. I was in heaven. On our last night in Holbox, I went into the kitchen with $50 USD in my pocket to tip the crew for our excellent meals. I had to duck. A giant parrot swooped over my head as it flew from one side of the kitchen to the other. The parrot was their pet. I watched it swoop and shit directly into the food being prepared. I decided that a smiling "muchas gracias" and a handshake for each of the people in the kitchen was better than giving them the $50, which I might need later to pay for my de-worming or whatever else you might get from eating bird shit.

The second day out was much the same as the first and I think the second boat also turned around at the Contoy pass. Sunset that night was beautiful, but made me worry about tomorrow. It was hurricane and tropical storm season in Mexico, we were in the middle of nowhere and one could not just call the Coast Guard to come get you. What would tomorrow bring?

Tomorrow brought one of the most dangerous days of our lives. By the time we got to Isla Contoy and stopped at the reef pass, a storm was barreling in. The captain felt we could still make it. I felt we would be risking our lives. The other boat had turned around and headed back to Isla Contoy. There was a debate and I finally had to pull the "I'm the paying customer" card and insist that we duck back into the lee side of Isla Contoy and we did. The storm BLASTED us. There is no way that would not have been dangerous as hell at sea. But, like most tropical storms, it left quickly and sunny warm skies appeared again, so we launched back out to sea.

We did not try the ocean pass because the waves were so much bigger now due to the storm. We headed for the colder green water outside of Contoy. That water is cold and green because of upwellings of current from below. We found the most beautiful juvenile whale shark I have ever seen, surrounded by a school of small fish, swimming in the odd-colored water with lightning and rain storms all around. Eli and I decided to jump in. Eli had a gigantic and expensive video camera and in all the excitement, terror and rocking of the boat, it fell overboard and headed to the bottom. I have never seen a human react quicker. Eli was after that camera like a rocket and he got it. I followed and we both got great shots of the whale sharks and mantas in that very strange light and coloration of the sea. Finally, the lightning was getting too close and it was time to go.

The storm hit us as soon as we got on board. It was not like a rain storm; it was like a fire hose in your face. Our two friends, Isabelle and Ariana (we called them the Radio Twins because they never stopped talking and laughing...lifelong friends having the time of their lives in Mexico), finally noticed that I had gone silent. They called me the CEO, because I was a recently retired CEO. Isabelle said, "Hey, has anyone noticed that the CEO has gone silent on us?" as the rain poured down so hard that I actually had on my face mask and snorkel to breathe more easily. She then observed that I had put on my wetsuit and had shoved all the water bottles I could find into that suit.

By now, the pouring rain and wind had completely drowned our two motors. That left us adrift, twenty or more miles out to sea, with no radio, no ability to point the pointy end of the boat into the oncoming waves and wind, no pump to pump out the water that was now filling up the interior of the boat—we were, in other words, screwed. I looked over at Eli and said to him, "On the danger scale of one to ten, where do you think we stand at the moment?" His answer, "We are at a nine." I then asked him if the only reason we were not at a ten was that we were not yet swimming, and he nodded his head in agreement. That quieted the party down.

I was dressing up in all my swim gear because I expected that Linda and I and the rest of us would be swimming soon...in the Gulf of Mexico....in a storm... with no one having any idea where we were. I filled my wet suit with water bottles because we would all need the water and the empty bottles would help us stay afloat. I had every intention of making it to the beach...eventually...and hoped to have everyone on that boat with me.

Since I am not currently dead, you can figure out that we survived. The storm passed completely. We could not see land in any direction, but the crew had a compass that worked. The radio did not work. One of the two engines still did not work. The other engine they primed with fresh fuel they had on board for emergencies and it sputtered along at about one-third speed, getting us home about six hours after we should have gotten home. The family of the crew and most of the town were out to meet us as we tied up, many of them crying. We were as lucky as could be and hungry enough to have another lobster and parrot shit pizza.

Toward the end of that trip, I pointed to a good-sized island in the distance and asked what island that might be. It was Isla Mujeras. I asked Eli if it would be possible to launch from Isla Mujeras in the future and he was already checking into that possibility. We have been on several whale shark adventures with Eli since them...all safer and easier than our Holbox trip and all launching from Isla Mujeras. Eli is always looking for ways to make his excursions safer and better for his devoted customers/friends. We highly recommend him and his amazing expeditions.

P.S....now that Linda and I actually know what we are doing with our underwater camera gear and know how to put on fancy swim fins, our photography on these trips rocks. Nothing is more fun than shooting right down the throat of an oncoming 45-foot-long sea creature with its mouth wide open. This is especially hard for those of us who live in Hawaii to believe, because we have whale sharks here as well, but we rarely see them and when we do it is usually just one or two. We have had days in the open ocean well off Isla Mujeras when we have been in the water with perhaps as many as 600 whale sharks at a time...along with dozens of pelagic manta rays and hundreds of other rays. Quite a sight.

CHAPTER FIFTEEN

When the Grandkids Hit Twelve Years of Age We Take Them Anywhere in the World They Want to Go, First Class, for a Month

My segue to this part of the book is that we are scheduled to take our granddaughter to Mexico with us this summer for whale sharks, but the new coronavirus has brought that trip into question.

Our two kids and their spouses, Jim and his wife Sarah and Stephanie and her husband Joe, have given us five grandchildren, The grandkids are Sam, Zach and Julia Hurzeler and Ava and Nathan Stanczak. Ava was the first to hit twelve and Nathan hit twelve this past summer...so we have two "grandkid trips" down and three to go. The second youngest told us at age four that he wanted to go to St. Louis...so that should be easy. The youngest was just born and we will be in our 80s when she hits twelve, so we are hoping she will want to go to Walmart for the afternoon.

Ava wanted to go to Europe. We did it in grand style. She wanted to see Harry Potter Theme Park England in London, and I told her no, but that we would make it up to her. When we pulled into St. Pancras Renaissance Hotel London her eyes lit up—she recognized that parts of the Harry Potter movies were shot at that hotel. Our first night in town, Chris Knight (my croc and shark dive buddy) joined us for dinner. Chris had been a Death Eater in the Harry Potter movies and Ava knew that...she was stoked. Helps that Chris is a big, strong, good-looking guy with a great smile. Ava enjoyed his company, as did Linda and I.

From London we headed to Paris on the Chunnel train under the English Channel. Paris was beautiful...I was not. I got about as sick as I have ever been. I was so sick I could not even make it to the hospital...throwing up and the trots to excess. I finally woke everyone up at two in the morning the second day and told them to get us a cab...we needed to get to the American Hospital in Paris immediately. We did and they fixed me up...saved the trip.

Lots of cool adventures in England, France, Germany, Switzerland and Italy.... with me driving all the way, starting from Paris and returning there. When we reached Venice, Italy, I got lost. We had three GPS apps working, each one telling me to go different ways. Lost, very lost. We ate up so much time that Ava and Linda needed to find a bathroom. We were out in some fields, God knows where, on a Sunday, so everything was closed anyway, no bathrooms in sight. It was then that Ava got the unusual opportunity to take a leak in a field with her grandmother. She is probably still in counseling to overcome that trauma.

Venice was amazing, as always. We stayed in a ridiculously expensive hotel in a room so luxurious that we had our own elevator. They fussed over us at check-in, providing young Ava with an experience like none she had ever had before. At one point, they about fell over themselves apologizing as they noticed me looking at something on the check-in desk that they had forgotten to offer me. They reached over and picked up a beautiful white mint with some tongs, dipped it in water and gave it to me. I popped it in my mouth. The people behind the counter were horrified. I had mistaken a rolled-up hand towel for a mint. I pulled it out of my mouth like you might pull out a towel for drying your hands in the bathroom. Ava laughed the hardest she has ever laughed in her life. The next morning they had a sign next to the towels making it clear in English that they were "Refreshing Hand Towels." I asked the guy behind the counter if that was the Don Hurzeler memorial sign and he just nodded. So much for impressing the grandkid.

We returned to Paris by way of the south of France. Ava's mom had made several trips to Grasse, France, to live with a family there, and we are still in touch with that family and saw them as recently as a few months ago. Ava got to visit them and the house that her mom lived in as a child. It was a very meaningful stop for us. Our daughter's counterpart in these student exchanges, Renaud, was married this past summer and you can find the best wedding photo I will ever take and the story of that photo on my website.

We also stayed in Monaco so Ava could understand that there are various layers of "rich" in this world. Loved Monaco.

As we left Paris for home, we had breakfast at United Airlines' Red Carpet Club...a private club you pay to join. I fly a lot and have been a member for decades. It was there that Ava learned what a sick and twisted person I am. She noticed me leaning over to read the name tag on a briefcase. Later, when we were in line to gather up breakfast, she watched me engage the guy who owned that briefcase. I get bored when I travel and invented this little game solely for the purpose of amusing me and me only. I got the guy's attention and said, "Oh, my gosh...it's Winston Cliveborne of IBM...I have not seen you since about five years ago at home office." The guy turned to me with that look of "who the hell are you?" and "oh, I am going to try to pretend I know you." I love that look. Before he could say anything I said, "Don Hurzeler...I was one of the keynote speakers there and you and I had dinner afterwards." That changed his look to "oh, my gosh...now I remember...so good to see you," handshakes all around. Never met that guy in my life...just wanted to trigger that phony reaction and then chuckle to myself.

Unknown to me, Ava watched this whole thing. Once we got our coffee and food, we returned to our table and Ava said to me...and I quote, "You were just fucking with that guy....right?" Yup...I was just fucking with him. She seemed to get it and it tickled her no end. I told her the best was yet to come.

So, the guy's now in the terminal...I was this guy before I got good and retired. Busy as could be on the phone, bossing around people by cell phone just loud enough for everyone around him to hear, not caring who he might be disturbing....yup, I was that guy. So, as that guy half yelled at some poor person on the other side of the conversation, he had his back to the screen updating the status of upcoming flights. I noticed his name was on the upgrade list...like I said, I was him at one point and I knew that getting upgraded would be important to him. He continued with his back turned as his name made its way up the upgrade list. When it reached the top and he got upgraded, I told Ava to follow along as I went in for the kill. I walked over to him and interrupted his phone call. He tried to be polite and put his hand over the phone to listen to me for a moment. I reminded him that I was in charge of United Airlines operations world-wide (complete bullshit...I never worked for any airline a day in my life) and that I had instructed them to move him up to first class on his upcoming flight (which was not our upcoming flight) and that any time in the future—forever, he needed a free upgrade to just mention my name. He was speechless. We left. He ran over, grabbed his upgrade, waved his thanks to me and boarded his plane. I only wish I could have been there as he tried to remember my name or, better yet, remembered my name and insisted he was to be upgraded for free on his very next flight. Ava now knew the true me...and she was very impressed, as am I much of the time.

We cherished our time with beautiful Ava in Europe...one of the best months of our lives (with the exception of the getting sick part and the electronic speeding ticket I got while driving through Lyon, France, for going exactly three kilometers over the speed limit...said ticket now residing at the bottom of some trash dump here on this island.)

Nathan chooses Australia

Nate is a hell of an athlete and a great surfer. He, like Ava, has been in the water with Linda and me with sharks and has hiked out to the lava flow with us. He has been around us enough to know not to trust us fully, but he easily trusted us enough to head off to Australia with us.

We traveled throughout Australia with Nate...Sydney, Uluru, Cairns, Port Douglas, the Great Barrier Reef and elsewhere. He got to surf Manly Beach and watch Bondi Beach go off with twenty-foot surf. We explored remote places and kept him busy. He won $50 from me when I bet him that he could not swim off a boat we were on to the beach and back without getting eaten by a shark—it was an area well-known for shark attacks. He made it, struggling a little toward the end, but he got back on the boat smiling (in retrospect, I guess that does not qualify me for Grandfather of the Year).

The Great Barrier Reef was the highlight of the trip. We snorkeled several sections of the reef....one in such challenging current conditions that I hired a guide to make sure we got back to the boat alive, another in absolutely perfect conditions and a third in the Low Isles where visibility was low and shark counts were high. Each one an adventure.

On the Lower Isles stop, Nate swam over to me and asked me to give him my expensive camera and housing. I gave it to him and off he swam. When he came back, he gave me the camera and told me he got a great photo of a turtle that we may want to sell in the gallery. I said, "We will see," knowing full well that using a fisheye lens underwater for the first time was tricky business. Much to my surprise, when we put the image into the computer and blew it up to look for detail, it was an excellent photo. I did have one question. I asked him how he had dealt with that guy over on the right of the frame...a blacktip shark bigger than he was. Nate is not afraid of sharks at all, but that one surprised him. He never saw him in the water. I had seen him as he buzzed harmlessly by my legs and headed off toward Nate and the turtle. He did not look like he was any kind of a problem at all and he was not. Still, a good lesson for Nate to keep his eyes open and look around when he is in any ocean.

We spoiled Nathan for the rest of his life with first-class air travel. The trip back to Oahu had beds in first class and Nathan slept most of the way home. Fantastic. Once on Oahu, we were joined by family and friends to welcome Nathan home and to dine with Linda and me on the occasion of our 50th wedding anniversary. Quite a night.

Nathan also got to surf a couple of my favorite spots in the Waikiki area and then got to surf Pipeline and Backdoor in head high conditions...and he ripped it.

And now we have a few years to wait before Sam, Zach and Julia hit twelve. I am guessing Zach may change his mind on St. Louis. Wonder where the next three will want to go? Wherever it is, we will be with our grandchildren and that will be just perfect for us. Life is good.

CHAPTER SIXTEEN

An Assortment of Travel Adventures From Around the World

We've been to something like a hundred countries and we have lots more travel ahead, if our finances and health hold out—I am self-isolating at home so as not to get the novel coronavirus as I write this book. Most of our travel....normal stuff. But along the way...some oddities....

Egypt

A trip to Egypt where I foolishly allowed a guy at a fifth-rate zoo to put a very much alive king cobra around my neck. We were traveling with a bodyguard—it was in the days before one of the revolutions in Egypt and U.S. citizens were not thought to be safe there at that time. I had stepped away from him to check out that zoo and told him what I had done when he found me. He turned pale. I assured him that it was defanged and harmless. He informed me that it was fully-fanged and that "zoo" was a place where they milked cobras for their venom. Seemed like a nice enough snake to me.

We drank a fresh sugar cane concoction made by a street vendor friend of our bodyguard. The drink included dirty-looking sugar cane in a blender with some nice Nile water. Linda was the first to fall deathly ill. The bodyguard and I went to a pharmacy and explained her symptoms. The pharmacist pulled out three different medicines...all made in the U.S., all unopened and shrink-wrapped, all unexpired and as it turned out later, all completely appropriate for what ailed her (as verified by our own doctors when we got home). Total charge for the consult and the meds....three U.S. dollars.

But I wanted her to see a real doctor, like right now. So, the bodyguard got ahold of a doctor who said he would see her at his office in four hours and the charge would be $150 cash. I told the bodyguard I wanted him to come here...now...and I would pay him $50 USD cash. He was there in ten minutes.

The doctor was Muslim and would neither look at nor speak to Linda. He did, however, do a professional job of checking her over and then gave her a couple of shots and told me to tell her to take the medicines the pharmacist had given her. Surprisingly, she got much better quickly.

Next up...I got sick. I was out in the middle of the Nile on a hot day in one of those odd little ancient-looking sail boats. I had the bodyguard with me. At one point I told him to flag down one of the speed boats on the river, pay them whatever he had to and get me back to the Nile cruiser we were on that was docked in Luxor for the day. He waved one down right away, paid the guy a few dollars and got me back to the dock. I told him I would be okay to walk the hundred yards back to our ship, but he would have none of it...said he would stick with me. Good thing...I made it ten more steps, threw up and passed out in the street.

Half hour later, here comes my Muslim doctor friend. Checks me out. Shoots me up. Gives me some meds. I explain to him that we have five....count them, five...airplane trips in Egypt the very next day. Neither Linda nor I wanted to be traveling while throwing up or having diarrhea. I told him to shoot us full of concrete or whatever...anything as long as we could make it from Luxor to Cairo to Abu Simbel to Cairo to Sharm El-Sheikh...with one other stop I cannot currently recall. He smiled and reached for his bag of tricks. One more shot for both Linda and me and $50 more U.S. dollars in his pocket. Hell of a doctor actually. We traveled for nearly sixteen hours the next day without incident.

Things are a bit lax in Egypt. Case in point, a snorkel trip we took to Ras Mohammed Marine Reserve. We were on a boat with the most snorkelers I ever saw on one boat...maybe 150. Two Americans...us. 148 Russians. I doubted that any of them had ever snorkeled. The official photographer for the boat spoke English well and I mentioned to him that we were experienced snorkelers and would like to get in early. He not only agreed, but said that it was about to become a zoo and he would like to get some photos of us before the horde hit the water.

The second I hit the water, a large and aggressive oceanic whitetip shark took a very hard charge at me. Oceanic whitetips are dangerous damn sharks. The boat's photographer told me that he saw them every day and they never bothered anyone and asked us not to mention the encounter as everyone would then be too afraid to get in the water. Before I could answer, the sound of a hundred or more flailing snorkelers surrounded us. Much to my surprise, the shark disappeared.

Read up on shark attacks at Sharm El-Sheikh. We were there in late 2009... some of the most beautiful snorkeling on earth. However, in 2010 there were at least four attacks by oceanic whitetip sharks, and three Russians and a German were killed or badly injured. One attack was just feet off the beach at the resort... like ten feet from shore.

Egypt was one of the most interesting places Linda and I have ever visited. If you wait until it is safe to go, you may never get to see it. We traveled with an armed bodyguard, in local clothes, in a nondescript private car, by ourselves for nearly a month. We easily bribed our way into places we could not believe we got to see. Were welcomed in mosques and homes and hotels, each one more interesting than the last. Got to see basically the whole country and parts of another country or two we were not really allowed to enter. It was a hell of an adventure.

Our flight home took us from Cairo to Frankfurt, Germany. The Egyptian businessman two rows in front of us appeared to sleep through the early morning flight. I say appeared because he was quite dead when I tapped him on the shoulder to let him know it was time to get up and exit the plane. Instead, he just fell over into the aisle...dead as a doornail. Linda and I have always been highly suspicious that the guy in the seat right in front of us and right behind him had something to do with him dying...but I will save that for another book. Strange trip indeed.

St. Kitts

Linda and I visited St. Kitts on a cruise designed to take us to many of the Caribbean islands that few people visit. We found information about a beautiful snorkeling beach and got a cab to take us there. We arranged for the driver to return in three hours to pick us up. Should have made that three minutes. The snorkeling was terrible and dangerous. We retired to a beach bar.

So, seated at the beach bar, Linda enjoying a beer and me a Coke, and there is no one else around. Then, looking down the beach I spot an old woman coming our way. She eventually makes it to the bar and sits down next to us. We strike up a conversation.

She asks where I like to travel. I mention Big Sur as a favorite. She smiles and asks if I have a favorite place in Big Sur...I do, Nepenthe restaurant, been going there since it opened in the 1950s. I asked her if she had ever been. She had, the owner was her godfather. I will never know why, but I immediately asked her if she had ever met the author Henry Miller. Mr. Miller wrote books of big interest to teenagers when I was a kid, like Tropic of Cancer. She had met Henry Miller. Then she smiled and mentioned that she was his mistress and had traveled with him on a book signing tour of London and Europe.

Did you see that episode of Seinfeld where Elaine is hating the time she has to spend with an old lady...until she asks the old lady if she had ever done anything interesting in her life and the lady answers that she had been the mistress of Gandhi? Yup...it was kind of like that.

That night I tracked down my cousin David Kahne. David was producing an album for Paul McCartney at the time and was living in London. He too is a big fan of Henry Miller and quite like a brother to me. I called him with my exciting news. Long silence. I asked him if he had heard me. He had. I asked what was wrong. Nothing, he said, other than the fact that he was in London that morning and had bought a first-edition copy of Henry Miller's *Tropic of Cancer,* signed by the author on that trip to London so many years ago. I don't believe in coincidence...and that was a strange one.

Peru

I completely love Peru. One of the most interesting countries on earth. Just a couple of quick items from our time there...

Linda and I showed up at the palace of the president of Peru only to find it surrounded by armed military and water cannons. Seems there was some kind of coup going on. I had Linda go stand between the soldiers so I could take her photo. The soldiers were not amused, nor was Linda. I then approached the guardhouse to the palace to find out what was going on. A guard explained it was basically a show of force against rumors of a coup...not to worry. I explained I was not worried at all, but I was disappointed because I actually wanted to meet the president and see the inside of the palace. Linda and I were somewhat surprised when he said, "Follow me." In we went.

I would like to tell you that we got to have a nice chat with the president...we did not...he was busy trying to quash a rebellion. We were served tea, given a nice tour and had our photo taken with some kind of dignitaries. Hey...you don't ask, you don't get. Turned out to be a great day for a near coup.

I gambled that night in a casino in Lima. Every time I won a small jackpot, they brought me my money and a plate of rice and beans. I have no idea why I got the rice and beans, but I love rice and beans and enjoyed the evening.

The next day, we hired a driver with a good car and a guide. We wanted to go see the house that Nobel Prize winning poet Pablo Neruda once lived in on the coast of Peru. They picked us up at the hotel and mentioned to us that we were spending a lot of money for this trip. Would we consider adding one more person to the large car and splitting the cost? Deal. They drove to pick her up. She got in the car and spoke to the guide in Spanish. As soon as she stopped talking, I got her attention and asked her what canton in Switzerland she lived in. She asked how I could tell she was Swiss when she had only spoken Spanish up to that point. I told her I use to work in Zurich and her accent sounded familiar. She worked in Zurich. I told her I had recently retired from Zurich Financial Services. She worked for Zurich Financial Services...in fact, it turned out she worked for a good friend of mine. Small world...and this new acquaintance saved me a bunch of money.

Okay...this one will not show me in my best light, and my wife still hates me for it. Lima has a museum of ancient art...Peruvian art, mostly ceramics and statues and jewelry. It is beyond interesting . I believe it is called the Museo Larco and I highly recommend it.

Right next door to the main gallery is another gallery of the museum dedicated to much the same kind of art, but all of it with an erotic theme. By erotic, I thought Henry Miller had a pretty dirty mind, but you should see this stuff. High-grade, really well-done professional-looking art that is just jaw-droppingly pornographic... proudly and openly displayed.

Here comes the bad part...keep in mind this was years ago before I was "woke" or had any sense whatsoever (in fact, I would go back and apologize today if that were possible). And if the lady in question is, by some mind-boggling chance, reading this passage, I do profusely apologize. Shame on me.

We had a lovely young lady acting as docent for us in the erotic museum. Although she was young and I was not, she was about a lifetime more mature than I. She would show us something hideous and give us some of its history and then move on to the next object that should have been viewed in a booth after dropping in a quarter or whatever they charge these days. I should have just left it at that, but I could not. She would conclude her little talk and I would say something like "excuse me, I don't understand, can you tell me again exactly what that monkey is doing to that lady bent over in front of him?" She would then explain and I would follow up with something like "but how is that even possible, I thought that was an exit not an entrance." Linda put up with this one time, kicked me hard in the shins, gave me the dirtiest look she could muster and left the museum. I followed just twenty minutes later.

We were told several times never ever to get in a cab in Lima. The instructions were clear. But at one point we went on a long walk to see the city. All was going well until a gun fight broke out. We found cover and I told Linda I was going to get us a cab....told her I had a plan...and I did. I waited until some poor old guy of about 80 came by driving a cab and I jumped out in front of him. We got in and he took us all the way across town for just $3. My plan was...he was 80 and I figured I could take him and hijack the cab if I had to...didn't have to...he was a perfect cab driver.

When we arrived in Cusco, Peru, we were met not by the one armed bodyguard I had hired, but two. Two guys on opposite sides of the baggage area holding up signs with our name. There is not much oxygen in the 12,000 foot high city of Cusco, so I was already confused. I looked them over carefully and picked the one that felt right to me. I asked him a couple of questions and he had the right answers. I mentioned the other guy and he said not to worry, he would not have let us go off with him as he was a well-known kidnapper. Welcome to Cusco.

We were headed from Cusco to Machu Picchu. You can hike there if you wish (seems pretty stupid to me) or you can take a nice train or a really nice train. We decided on the really nice train. Not so fast...the bodyguard told us that all the trains had gone on strike, but not to worry, he would get us on the first one out once the strike was over in a day or two....happens all the time. He had arranged for a great tour for us the next day and it was, in fact, a fantastic tour of the area.

Two things about the tour. It started at 6:30 a.m. in Cusco. Since I had tried chewing coca leaves the night before and I had not slept one minute, I was up and raring to go...just as soon as I chewed a whole bunch more of those leaves. (Turns out cocaine is made from coca leaves.) So at 6:31 a.m., some Peruvian guy with the kind of camera that crime reporters used in about 1946 took our photo as we staggered through Cusco. I waved him off and he left.

In between stops, the driver would let a vendor get aboard the bus and he had from that point to the next stop to make his sale of...coca leaves (yes, I will take the large bag, please), or odd-looking hats with tassels hanging down the sides (already have one, thanks), or the most bizarre item of the day, a fermented alcoholic drink. I knew this guy had not been making any sales on any of the other buses all day because he got on the bus sweating like Elvis and nervous as could be. He launched into his broken English sales talk...commenting on the history of the product and its many benefits. He had yet to tell us what the product was. He then pulls out a giant bottle of liquid that looks like there is a storm going on inside....white and dark and swirling. He mentions, kind of quietly, that it is the fermented milk of the llama. I don't think anyone past our row heard what it was. He then took off the cap and the entire bus knew what it was instantly. What it was was VILE. I have never smelled anything like it and I use to live with a bunch of surfers. He then proceeded to offer anyone who wanted one to take a tug off that nasty-looking bottle. I looked around for Candid Camera. No sales on this bus either.

Late in the afternoon and some 150 miles away from where we had started, a guy came up to me as I got off the bus. It was the guy from 6:31 a.m. this morning in Cusco...the guy with the old reporter's camera. He handed me a nice-looking booklet. In the booklet was that early morning photo along with a photo of Linda and me at every stop along the way for that entire day. The photos were not bad and the booklet had scenes from our various stops along with some of the history of those places. I was astonished and would have bought it if for no other reason than to reward his hard work. He only asked five dollars, U.S. I gave it to him and shook his hand...told him how much I appreciated his work. Unfortunately, he had other tourists to sell booklets to; otherwise I was going to offer him a nice llama milk cocktail to cap off his day.

Chicago...welcome to the neighborhood

We moved from Southern California to Inverness, Illinois (near Chicago) in 1982. None of us wanted to make the move from the beach to the plains, but my new boss mentioned that my one-and-only-pay check would available there and only there. So, we packed up the house, two kids and a rabbit and made our way to our new home.

I moved Linda and the kids so the kids could get into their new school in time for a new school year. After moving them in, I returned to California where I was one of the people in charge of closing down a large office over the next six months. This was an office filled with my friends, the people who had taught me my trade, people I hired and people I loved. Those six months were difficult in many ways.

My old friend, London Bradley, was put in the same position, and having moved his family at the same time, he became my roommate in California for a half a year. We had a great time together and got the job done. London Bradley was a bit infamous...he was the NCAA referee whom Bobby Knight of Indiana had thrown the chair at during a game. We tried to never let London forget that moment.

The house in Inverness was spectacular by California standards. Lots of square feet, large lot, overlooking a lake, indoor running track that a neighbor, NFL star Walter Payton, came over to check out. Great neighbors all around and a beautiful area.

So...just a week into this new arrangement I get a call from Linda in Inverness. She wanted to know just what kind of a neighborhood I had put her and our two kids into. I asked her why she was bothering me with such a question...it was the most beautiful place we had ever lived. Turns out she was asking because earlier that night, as she was cleaning up after dinner, she looked out the window to see three black stretch limos slowly winding their way through the neighborhood... after dark, with their lights off. They stopped at the house directly across from her kitchen window. Five men in black trench coats got out of each limo and surrounded the house. They then produced shotguns from under the trench coats and proceeded to blow out every window in the two-story house. When they were done, they slowly got back in their limos and quietly drove out of the neighborhood.

For some reason, this bothered my wife and the two kids. Linda called the police, but the officers, who were just minutes away, did not show up for over an hour. The family who lived in that house across from our kitchen window were unharmed. However, they felt a need to move back to Sicily the very next morning, without even bothering to fix the windows.

We obviously never got to really know those folks next door. However, I am pretty sure that he was not exclusively in the food and beverage business that he said he had started after moving to Illinois from Sicily a few years earlier. Seemed like a heck of a nice guy. Must have pissed off someone.

That was our welcome to Chicago.

Las Vegas

For decades, I held a real job and was a professional gambler on the side. I stuck with big-dollar, no-limit poker and high-end ($5 to $100) slot machines. I didn't drink, didn't take any casino perks to keep me playing, didn't have a lot of time to spend in casinos, adhered to strict limits on my losses and walked out of the casino when I had big wins...like the night I won $87,500 on slot machines. I reported every penny of gain on my income taxes and paid those taxes. I kept detailed notes on my winnings and losses and I made exceptionally good money over the years as a gambler.

That said, I think gambling is for losers. I don't mean you are a loser if you gamble…I mean that every gambler I have ever known is eventually beaten by the math of casino odds. You can win and stay ahead, sometimes for quite a while. However, in the long run, the "house" wins. Gambling can make you feel and look like a winner, but then one night at 2 a.m. when you hit a losing streak and just can't walk away, the math of casino play surges past you and leaves you a loser. I have also noted that it is those who can least afford to lose that money that lose it first. Gambling is for winners only…that is how casinos make you feel. The truth is…gamble enough and you will become just another victim of the math of the odds.

The saddest ones are the ones I call the instant losers. I would see them hit $25,000 jackpots, go over and suggest to them that they go home right this second, circle around an hour later to see them still at the machines, ask them how they were doing and they would often tell me that they are now down $3000…as in, the $25,000 is gone and another $3000 on top of it…instant loser.

Gamblers have thousands of stories, as do I. However, I want to pass along just one….

Linda and I were in Las Vegas for an insurance industry event in which I had a key role. Unfortunately for me, the new worldwide CEO of my company had called for a command performance from me the next day in New York City. I already had the presentation prepared and knew my stuff…it was just a matter of getting to NYC and back that same day for an important dinner in Las Vegas…but it could be done.

So, I finished up a day in my room at the Las Vegas hotel. I had invited a new hire from San Diego to join me for the day for an orientation and so we could get to know one another a little better. At about 4 p.m., Linda joined us and told me it would soon be time for me to head to the airport. So I told Robert to stay the night and head home in the morning, then I began to walk him down to the lobby. Linda asked where I was going. I told her I was going to make sure he got a room and would be right back. Linda turned to Robert, whom she had just met that day, and said to him, "Robert, don't let Don gamble, it could ruin your life." This confused Robert no end and I explained that he should ignore her—she had probably gotten into the wine. We headed to the front desk. But wait…the route took us through the casino. At one point I stopped and told Robert to wait a minute. I put a ten-dollar bill in a two-coin $5 slot machine and spun it once. Up came the jackpot…worth $25,000. Robert came rushing over, pulling money out of his pocket, and said, "That looked pretty easy." I told him that was probably what Linda was talking about...I have always been just plain lucky and should never be looked to as a guide in these matters.

Robert went off to get his room. I called Linda and thought that she might want to see the fun of getting cashed out of a $25,000 jackpot. As I waited for her, I asked the cocktail waitress (cocktail waitresses are ALWAYS the first on the scene when a big jackpot has hit) how often that particular machine hit the big one. She said she had been there fourteen years and had never seen it hit before tonight.

About the time Linda arrived, so did a guy out of central casting for either The Sopranos or The Godfather. He was there to give me the cash, comp my room and entertainment, and extend my stay by a few days. I told him I wanted no comps of any kind and that I wanted a check. I did not tell him I was on my way to New York in about two hours and did not want to be carrying twenty-five big ones with me on the plane nor did I want to leave them with Linda to worry about. He explained that he could not write me a check, that they paid in cash. I explained to him that they could write me a check and I wanted that check now. He finally agreed to get me the check if I would follow him down into the depths of the hotel to the accounting office. This did not feel right, but off we went.

Once we got to the basement, this big thug put the hard sell on us to take the cash and the comps...they wanted me to play the money back into their hands. Got to admit that he scared both Linda and me, but in the end we did get the check, I did fly to New York City that night, and I gave the presentation in the morning and flew back in time for dinner in Las Vegas the following night. Quite a twenty-four hours. And, to the best of my knowledge, it did not ruin Robert's life. In fact, we are both long retired and remain friends to this day.

One other Las Vegas story...

I flew out to Las Vegas to be interviewed by the nominating committee of the Chartered Property and Casualty Underwriters Society in the hopes they would nominate me to go through the leadership chairs of the society, starting as secretary and advancing each year to the next higher chair, to end up as president of the 20,000-member volunteer organization. I loved the CPCU and had been a very active member for a couple of decades. This was probably going to be my only chance to get the nomination and the pressure was on. I put on my most serious-looking black suit, a red and gold power tie, my best shoes and a fancy watch. I felt that I looked presidential. Now I just had to convince a majority of the committee that I could be presidential.

I arrived in Las Vegas about two hours before the interview. I had no room...in and out in one day. The temperature was over 100 degrees and I was melting. I was also hungry. So I looked around for a healthy place where I could get some great food and found just the spot nearby....Baskin-Robbins 31 Flavors. Perfect.

I went to the store and got in line. The next-nicest-dressed person in line had on a bathing suit and a tee shirt. I kind of stood out. In a few minutes, I worked my way to the head of the line and put in my order...I wanted a chocolate milkshake. The lady behind the counter made my shake and told me I owed her $1.95. I could clearly see the sign behind her...there was only one size and price for a shake and that price was $2.95. Since the CPCU Society is founded on the bedrock of high ethical standards, I did not want to make a bad karma move and profit from her mistake. I said, "Thank you much, but the sign says $2.95 and I do not want to be accidently undercharged." Her reply, "No, $1.95 is the correct price....we give all the limo drivers a discount."

So much for feeling that I looked presidential.

However, the karma did treat me right. I opened my remarks to the committee with that story, it got a big laugh and I got the job. And the shake was delicious.

CPCU provided me with one other good laugh. My friend Michael was an important member of an important committee filled with top executives from the industry. I too was a member of that committee. The meetings were dead boring... always. I do not do well in such situations. And, by the way, this committee was filled with very serious people who probably had not laughed since movies became talkies (there is one for you to look up).

The most casual any of these meetings ever got was the rare occasion when one or more of the members risked actually taking off his suit jacket and continuing in the meeting in just his long-sleeved white shirt and tie. You are getting the picture... not your most fun-loving group.

So Michael took off his suit coat and hung it on the back of his chair. A break was called and most everyone headed off to the bathroom. I stayed behind. I took the huge name tag that Michael had on the front of his suit coat, turned it over to the unused side and printed in bold black Sharpie pen, "Ask Me About Amway Products." I then returned the name tag to the suit and sat back to wait for the fun that was sure to come when he put that coat back on and interacted with his fellow committee members.

By the boring end of the boring meeting, I had long since forgotten about the name tag. The meeting came to a close. Everyone stood up. Suit coats were put back on and, one by one, jaws dropped as the committee members looked over at Michael. How DARE he try to sell these aristocrats of the insurance business his petty Amway products? One after another shook his head in disgust, quickly moved away from Michael and exited the room. Not sure when Michael found out about the name tag. I, too, had left in disgust.

And just to show you that there is a God and karma works...here is how all that came back to bite me...

As a young insurance guy, I earned a Chartered Life Underwriter designation, CLU for short. It was like a CPA designation, only for life insurance professionals.

We only had one major life insurance company in Orange County, California, at the time...the Pacific Mutual Life Insurance Company in Newport Beach. Much to my surprise, that fine company invited me, an Allstate® Insurance employee, to come join them to celebrate my success. All of the new CLU designees from Orange County...about twenty of us...got similar invitations to have lunch with the chairman and board of directors of Pacific Mutual in the board room of their beautiful home office. I quickly accepted. I was getting very few invites to lunch with any chairmen of anything in those days.

Unfortunately, on the day of the lunch I was on a business trip in Reno, Nevada. After a breakfast meeting there, I flew to Las Vegas, changed planes and flew home to Orange County. Landed a little late. I was going to be late for the lunch.

I got in my car and raced the short distance to Newport Beach. I ran into the building and asked directions to the board dining room. I ran to the room and, drat, the door was closed and locked. I put my ear to the door and could hear the sounds of the group having lunch...utensils clinking and people talking. Decision time...do I just slink away and miss the lunch or do I knock on the door, apologize to one and all for my tardiness and enjoy the rest of the luncheon? I chose to knock.

Soon as I knocked, the entire room fell silent. Uh oh. I could hear someone coming to the door and then the door opened. A table away, the chairman of the company stood up and asked me what I needed. I explained that I was twenty minutes late for the new CLU lunch and that I very much apologized. He smiled, looked around the room and said, "Don't worry son, you are A WEEK and twenty minutes late for that lunch...it was last week. This is our regular board meeting." At that, the room rocked with laughter...me being the only exception. When things settled down, he asked me for my name. I assured him that I was not about to give him that information, apologized again and pretty much ran the hell out of there... leaving even more laughter behind.

Karma...it can be a bitch.

Paris on 9/11

Linda and I were in Paris on 9/11. We had just checked into the Paris Hilton... that is, the hotel with that name that is no longer there and not the social media person with that name. My assistant in Chicago called and told me what had just happened and then we, like the rest of world, turned on the TV.

We burned up the phone lines trying to contact important people in our lives and my boss, whose office looked directly across at the World Trade Towers. He was on the top floor of the One Liberty Plaza building, along with hundreds of our employees. CNN kept reporting that One Liberty Plaza was coming down (it did not).

Our company lost four employees in and around the World Trade Plaza, one of them a longtime friend. We had lived in the shadow of the towers and I had worked in the Financial District, so there were lots of my friends to try to locate... including my best friend, Mike Fayles. We also had a business to run, a big league commercial insurance business, and that business was in chaos. It was the worst of times.

I could fill a book about what went on that day and the days ahead, but so could you and all it would do is depress both of us. But I do want to mention one thing. This is something that I told all of my employees in writing and in a phone conference, as soon as that could be arranged...the world will remember you by how you treat our customers and each other in the days ahead. I was right about that...and I gave them plenty of leeway to do the right thing without asking for permission.

Which brings me to the Paris Hilton. After hours of being cooped up watching CNN and trying to make phone calls, Linda suggested we go for a walk to try to walk off some of the tension we both felt. We were close to the Eiffel Tower. Let's take a stroll over there, she said. Good idea. I grabbed our passports and some money and off we went.

When I opened the door to our hotel room, there was a man standing there with a machine gun. I threw my hands up in the air and did not say a word. He reacted quickly and assured me he was there to protect me and would be available to go with us anywhere we wanted to go in the city. He also showed us where they had positioned a sniper on a roof top to give us and other guests further protection, if necessary.

I asked how I deserved this kind of protection. He said my profile said I was an American CEO and an extremely loyal customer and that they had no idea if this attack was going to be carried out anywhere else in the world that Americans might be. They were going to keep me safe at no charge whatsoever.

There was a no-fly period after 9/11 that made it impossible to get home for several days. The hotel extended our stay at our preferred rates, comped us breakfast each morning, gave us access to their free drinks lounge and arranged for all the activities we needed to do during our stay. Someone from the front desk checked in on us twice a day to see if we needed anything.

That is how to take care of a customer in need. Hilton. I will never forget them.

CHAPTER SEVENTEEN

New York City...A Subway Shocker

Linda I moved to New York City and loved it. We had an apartment looking out at the Statue of Liberty with the World Trade Center just down the street. After a year there, we moved to 45 Wall Street, a very odd place to live at the time. Our apartment building was the first apartment or condo building established on Wall Street in over one hundred years. There were few retail establishments around... this was THE heart of the Financial District.

We had a large apartment and invited my aging folks to come visit from California. They flew out and called me from LaGuardia.... "Where are you?" they asked, upon arrival. I told them I did not own a car and to get a cab to our place. That did not go over well—they were way out of their element in NYC.

Once they arrived, they found me on the phone negotiating for a new job in Baltimore. The conversation went on and on and finally my wife insisted that I wrap it up for the day and greet my folks. Good advice, and I followed it. We quickly decided to go to Midtown so Dad could see a guitar shop he had only read about and wanted to visit. Off we went.

Wall Street had a subway entrance that looked like a gaping hole leading to the underworld. As we entered, the hot air and smell from the station let my parents know that they were no longer in California. You could see the concern in their eyes. Linda made the situation worse when she suggested that we play "Spot the

Rat" when we got to the platform. This was a game Linda and I played...winner was the first to spot any of the cat-sized rats that lived down there. My mom thought Linda was kidding. She was not.

When the train arrived, we all got on and headed to our seats. Just as I was about to sit down, I heard a horrible scream. I looked toward the door of the train and saw that a woman had fallen between the station platform and the train and was wedged in solidly. I knew that she was about to die. The train doors would close. The train would leave the station. The lady who had fallen would be spun to her death. This was the exact reason for the "Mind the Gap" signs you see all over the London subways.

Here was the problem—this woman could not see. She was blind. A very large, loud, blind woman was wedged between the platform and the subway car. A scene out of a nightmare.

I jumped up immediately. I guess I had my hands in my pockets because all of my money flew out of my pockets and across the floor. I grabbed at the door as it was closing, just moments before disaster struck. Someone grabbed the door on the other side. By now the blind lady was hysterical. She understood completely what had happened and the danger she was in. As we tugged at her to try to get her free the doors kept trying to close. Each time the doors moved, she would swing her cane around wildly trying to keep them from closing. One of those swings broke my nose. Another closed one of my eyes and knocked my glasses to the floor. She beat the daylights out of me with that cane.

All of a sudden, she popped up out of the space she was in and I was able to pull her into the car with me. The doors shut like nothing had ever happened and the train lurched forward. I reached out to steady her, grabbing her by the shoulders. The rest of the car was completely silent and transfixed by this entire episode. As I steadied her, I said "Thank God you are okay." She quickly replied, "God had nothing to do with it, you stupid shit. Now get the fuck out of my way." At that, she pushed me harshly aside, took one step forward onto my glasses that were still on the floor, crushed them to bits, and then moved on to the last seat in the car.

I staggered over to my wife and parents, one eye blackened and closed, blood running hard out of both nostrils and very much shaken. As I sat down, the other people on the train gathered up all my money and broken glasses and brought them over to me. I sat there in silence, a silence that was broken by my dad, who said, "Son, if it were me, I would go ahead and take that job in Baltimore." And...I did.

CHAPTER EIGHTEEN

Live on the Radio With Joan Rivers

In the 1990s, 45 Wall Street in New York City was a strange place to live, but Linda and I loved it. In fact, I loved almost everything about living in NYC—it had the best of everything, including radio. One day, I rented a car and was on my way to apologize to an insurance broker in New Jersey (we had screwed up on a deal of his). Had to rent a car...did not own one in the city. I was listening to Joan Rivers on her number-one-rated radio show. She was her normal crazy/funny self, and she also took calls. On this particular day, she had heard a rumor that Hillary Clinton was about to come out as a lesbian. Joan spoke directly to her own large following from the gay community and said something like "I have always been there for you. Have always helped you to raise funds or increase awareness. And now I need you. If any of you have ever had an affair with Hillary, call me now. I want all the details and I want them now before anyone else can break the story." She said this half-jokingly, but you could tell she was not kidding. She kept coming back to the request time after time. No calls.

Now, we were not especially politically-correct or advanced in our thinking about a lot of things back in the 1990s, but even then, this felt a bit wrong to me. First, I was quite certain that a person's sex life was a private matter. Second, I have always hated rumors...so unfair. Third, no one on earth would blame Hillary for getting back at Bill. And lastly, what would a "lesbian affair" have to do with anything anyway? So, it felt wrong to me, but I will admit it had me smiling.

I pulled over to the side of road in rural New Jersey and called Joan. I got the screener. I changed my voice to sound as much like a woman as I could. I explained that I had had a long affair with Hillary...was reluctant to talk about it...but dearly loved Joan and would help her out with specifics, dates, places and whatever else she needed...and I would do so right now live on the radio. I got passed right through to Joan.

Joan was pretty excited and thanked me profusely. She offered to speak to me off the air, but I told her this needed to come out and I was ready to share the information with the world. She asked some leading questions and I could tell my answers just about stopped her in her tracks. I tried not to get too specific, but gave her and the audience a clear understanding of the depravity and wanton behavior that Hillary and I had enjoyed for many years. She bought it hook, line and sinker. Finally she said, "To tell you the truth, I never suspected Hillary Clinton of this kind of behavior...I am just speechless." I said, "Hillary Clinton....what does Hillary Clinton have to do with it?" A moment of silence and then she said, "You are speaking of Hillary Clinton...right?" I said, "Hell no. I thought you meant Sir Edmund Hillary (famous for being first to climb Mt. Everest). I had an affair with him for years. Hillary always wanted to wear his climbing gear to bed and always called me his sweet little sherpa."

At that point she laughed...just a little...and said, "I'm hanging up on you now...no one gets more laughs than me on this show," and the phone went dead.

I laughed all the way to the broker's office, but the laughter ended there. We really had screwed up and the broker tore me to shreds. Life in the big city—I loved it.

God bless Joan...I miss her.

CHAPTER NINETEEN

Staying Sane, Often at the Expense of Others

So I will conclude with the one thing that has kept me sane in times of stress, overwork and trouble...my childish, stupid and sometimes bizarre sense of humor. My sense of humor is not always generous. It is designed to amuse me and me only and I am a near complete success in that regard. I crack me up even when others just look at me and stare.

A couple of examples...

The Hurzeler Christmas Letter

One of my best friends, my college roommate Jack Nester, often tells me, "Whatever is wrong with you is no small thing." He says it jokingly, but I know he means it. There is something wrong with me and it has been wrong with me for a long time.

My early influences in the area of thought and writing were not Hemingway, Dickins, Kafka or Proust...they were *Mad Magazine, The Onion, National Lampoon* and a quadriplegic cartoonist named John Callahan. I graduated from *Mad Magazine* in my early teens, but found other writers who were edgy, mean-spirited and willing to make fun of anything and anyone, no matter how politically incorrect. They were kind of like the now-deceased comedian Don Rickles—it was okay to trash someone as long as you trashed everyone, including yourself. I see the stupidity and immaturity of that now, but the influence was deep and lasting. So, as you shake your head at the shameful writing that follows, please know that it came from another time...way before I was "woke" and became the better person that I am today. I say that because I should, not because it is true. Truth is I am still putting this garbage out to my long-term audience of readers, some of whom throw parties and read it to their friends, and others of whom who promptly throw the letters in the trash where they belong without ever reading them.

The Hurzeler Christmas Letter debuted in 1975. It was first sent out as a reaction to the fact that I was getting a lot of Christmas letters back then, most of which I loved and appreciated...but a few of which spent the entire letter letting me know how successful they had become and how talented their little shits...I mean children...were. Those last ones are the ones that prompted my first, quite odd, Hurzeler Christmas Letter. I have put one out every year since then...44 years' worth up to the latest one (at the time of the writing of this book in 2020).

You will see in a moment what makes these Christmas letters cringe-worthy and different. I never spend more than ten minutes writing them. They are always two pages. I never give the endeavor a moment's thought before I start the letter. They just flow out like dirty water and then I read them to my poor wife. She is my indicator of whether or not they have some limited humor or interest to them (trust me, I always find them funny as hell). Linda is also the one who, each year, says, "Wait a minute, you CANNOT put that in there," advice that I sometimes follow.

I usually place the letters inside the cheapest and most uninteresting Christmas card I can find....often in another language....so cheap they are sold by the pound. I address the envelopes, seal them, put stamps on them and then spread them out on my driveway. I drive my pickup over and over them until the tire marks are quite noticeable. Then I put them in the post. Every so often, I take the regular Christmas cards that people have sent me, cross out their names, put in our names and place them in a regular envelope for delivery...after the required thrashing from my pickup. As to the date I send them...I make sure it varies every year...as early as Thanksgiving and as late as February. The February ones give my readers the hope that I have finally given up on this fool's mission. I have not.

Every now and again I will hear a comic on TV using one of my lines from the Christmas letter. This really pisses me off, until I stop to take the time to remember that I stole the line from that comic to begin with.

Rather than bore you with forty-four yeas of this trash, and in an effort to cover up the fact that a HUGE amount of my writing is just plain painfully unfair/

poor/unfunny/space filler, I have decided to share just one sample letter with you, just enough to make you glad you never got one of these pieces of trash in the mail from me.

Here goes....this is a typical Hurzeler Christmas Letter...

Greetings from the Lazy Eye Ranch in Lake in the Hills, Illinois,

Well, Don's breast implants turned out to be a big mistake. The basic idea was sound. Don wanted to regain the athletic upper body look that he enjoyed as in his youth. Unfortunately, his 44D bust is more perky than athletic and "perky," covered in dark thick hair, turns out to not be a good look.

Linda is doing well in her new business. She runs a dental scrimshaw service. Linda will come to your home and carve whaling scenes into your natural teeth. The effect is unique, individualized and sure to cause a sensation. A number of her clients have specifically mentioned the "sensation" part.

This is Jimmy's first year as a high school senior. He dissected a frog in class the other day. The class was English Literature and the other students and teacher were horrified, as was the frog.

Stephanie is now in her senior year of Charm School. Next semester will be her last. She will be taking classes in listening, table setting and alternatives to the Farmer's Wipe. She is already charming as heck. Graduation is in June and then she hopes to land a high-paying job in the Charm industry.

Here is a riddle they taught her last semester: "What large animal has an asshole in the middle of its back?" Give up? The answer is Saddam Hussein's horse. See...I told you she was charming.

Our Catalog O'Inventions is just about ready for press. This year's new products include...

The Coach Passenger's Pal. An expandable porta potty that fits neatly in your purse or brief case. Perfect for when you are stuck in that middle seat on a long international flight. Folds down flat once used, although not quite as flat as before use. Includes instructions for diverting attention such as "wow...they must have burned the okra." Or "smells like they ran over some dog poop on takeoff." Available in brown only.

The At-home Tonsil Remover Kit. No more co-pays or time wasted in a hospital. Kit includes a wire snag, lighted mirror, foot-long styptic pencil and easy-to-follow (up to a point) instructions.

The Doctor Kevorkian Indoor Fogger. Just turn the nozzle and exit the room. Quickly fills the room with pleasant smelling, but highly-poisonous and lethal gas. Available in two convenient sizes, Grandma's Room and Double-Wide.

Mint-Scented Suppositories. Shove a few of these up your butt after a big greasy Mexican meal and turn yourself into a room deodorizer. Also available in Sea Breeze and Pine Forest.

1-900-BARK-4-ME. We also started a 1-900 telephone service for dogs. For the one-time low sign-up fee of just $25 and then just $1.99 per minute, your discerning dog gets an inflatable human leg and access to a bevy of bitches on our talk line for your dog's pleasure. We call it, Doggy Style.

In Other News...

Linda slipped into a deep trance after dinner (totally unrelated to the two bottles of wine she consumed) and awoke hours later with these amazing predictions...

- Wall Street will be renamed Double Rainbow Street to try to regain the confidence of the investing public.

- A tall man with a head the size and color of an orange will become the elected Premier of France.

- Schools across America will go back to the basics and start to teach gooder English.

- Hallmark will come out with a six-month calendar for senior citizens.

- Barbara Bush will replace George Washington on the one-dollar bill and no one will notice.

- The Memphis Art Museum will learn that their "Sweating Elvis in Concert" black velvet painting is a forgery.

- Alka-Seltzer® will introduce its product in suppository form and later have to admit that it was all meant to be a joke. By then it will be their top-selling product in Northern California.

- Ex-Vice President Dan Quayle will author a new book entitled Me Memories.

Which reminds me....a blind guy walks into a bar with a Chihuahua on a leash. The bartender says, "You can't bring a dog into my bar." The blind guy says, "That is my seeing-eye dog." The bartender says, "You have a Chihuahua for a seeing-eye dog?" The blind guy says, "They gave me a fucking Chihuahua?"

And one last update...Snowflake the Wonder Dog remains quite dead. Rest well, our formerly fur-covered friend.

Linda and I wish you a Merry Christmas or Happy whatever it is that you otherwise foolishly celebrate that will eventually lead you to the burning depths of Hell.

Respectfully,

Don, Linda, Jimmy and Stephanie Hurzeler and Snowflake the quite dead Wonder Dog

Okay...sorry to put you through that. Just wanted you to see an example of how I have wasted precious minutes of my life and validate my roomie's observation that there is something seriously wrong with me.

CHAPTER TWENTY

Pranks and Oddities at Work

I want to tell you a few stories from my work life that have absolutely nothing to do with anything in this book. In each case, this was just me trying to have fun at work...nothing to be proud of...some are pretty childish...some are kind of mean... all are completely true and I love them.

The story of Stan and the phone

Stan was a terrific guy. He was much older than I. Pretty serious. A good sense of humor, which he kept buried most of the time. I felt it was my job to help him express that sense of humor.

Our desks were on the second floor looking out on a four-lane street with an orange grove on the other side. There were telephone poles on the orange grove side of the street and there were often people up those poles working on the lines.

One day I noticed that the phone company had built one of those little tent-like things up near the top of the pole to protect the worker from the elements as he did what must have been extensive repairs on the telephone equipment and lines at that location. I also noticed that Stan seemed very interested in the work going on across the street. So...I called Stan. I told him that I was the repairman across the street and said that we were working on a report of trouble on his line.

Stan noted he had some problems with the line and would be happy to help the repairman in any way he could. No help needed now...I, I mean the repairman, told him...but he would call back if he needed Stan's help.

I waited five minutes. The entire five minutes Stan watched that tent to see if anything was happening. Nothing.

After five minutes, I called again and again pretended to be the repairman. I told him that the line seemed fine...the problem must be with the phone itself. Could he please disconnect the phone, come across the road and let me take a look at it. Stan fell for it hook, line and sinker.

Stan unplugged the phone and hurried down the stairs and across the street. I quickly filled in the two dozen of us who worked around him so we could all join in the fun. We all unplugged our phones and gathered near the big windows at the front of the building facing the telephone lines and the repairman.

Stan ran across the street. He positioned himself right under the little tent that was at the top of the telephone pole, yelled up to the repairman, and held his phone over his head. In just a few seconds, the repairman's head popped out of the tent. Words were exchanged. The repairman looked across the street...said something to Stan...and Stan turned to look back at us. We all waved our phones at him and that was that. Stan came storming back toward the building. The repairman gave us a big thumbs-up and a smile...and we plugged in our phones and all got back to work. When Stan arrived, he just stood there...phone in hand...and looked around for the guilty party. After about a minute of our ignoring him, tight-assed Stan broke out laughing and said, "I've got to admit...you got me with that one." Mission accomplished.

My $1200-a-bottle brandy

Linda and I moved to Pittsburgh in about 1981. We bought a modest 8000-square foot house there in a beautiful location. We moved in on a Wednesday and on Friday we had about 50 people from my office...employees and spouses...over to the house for a party. I had the whole thing catered. Hired a chamber orchestra to play classical music on the bridge that connected one part of the second story to another (that wasn't a big hit with the people I had invited over...they were more the Steelers-fan type than the chamber-orchestra type). I hired a bartender and told him to serve absolutely anything he could find in our bar, the good stuff and the good wine included.

The party was a big success. We all got to know one another and a good time was had by all. Every single person leaving the party thanked me for letting them experience "the brandy." Best brandy they had ever drunk. They loved it. "Thank you, Mr. Hurzeler." The group was pretty young and I guess they had never had any brandy. Apparently they found my brandy and everyone tried it...and liked it A LOT.

As soon as the last guest left, I ran into the room where we had set up the bar and asked the bartender about the brandy. He apologized profusely. He said it kind of got away from him and before he fully realized what he had done, the guests had drunk up all the brandy. He also reminded me about five times in thirty seconds that I had said it was okay to serve ANYTHING he found in the bar.

Now I was curious. I asked him to show me the brandy he had served. He almost tried to hide the box of empty bottles from me. I reached over and picked one up. He said, "Sir, I am just so sorry." And well he should have been...each bottle had the price tag still on it...$1200.

This guy had served my guests an entire case of $1200-a-bottle brandy.

My mind went on rinse cycle. How could this have happened? How could I have been so stupid as to have put out my $15,000 case of brandy for my guests to clean out in just a few hours? And then the little light went on for me. I remembered where I had purchased the brandy. I had bought it in Tijuana, Mexico. It didn't cost $1200 a bottle. It cost $$1200 a bottle...that is, 1200 pesos a bottle...about one dollar and twenty cents. You could have used this stuff to start the barbecue—it was some of the nastiest rotgut "brandy" ever manufactured. Presidente Brandy. I was lucky I didn't blind my entire office.

I never told them the real cost of the brandy. Why? Because as far as I was concerned, it was priceless.

Paging all porno patrons

Several of us low-level managers got called up to the West Coast Zone Office of the company to participate in a training seminar. I checked into the hotel and went for a long run. On the way back to the hotel I noticed three of my fellow managers entering a porno theater. They were away from home and why not do something they could never get away with at home...go see a dirty movie. Their names will be left out to protect the guilty.

Well...this was just too good a setup to let pass. I waited 15 minutes and called the manager of the theater. I told him we had a business emergency, gave him "my" name (I gave him the name of the Zone vice president) and asked him to please interrupt the movie and ask for...and I gave him the names of my three buddies who it turned out were sitting all together in the front row. Unbelievably, this guy shut off the movie, turned up the house lights, went to the front of the stage, mentioned the name of the Zone VP and said he had a message for—and then he named the three guys sitting right there. No one moved, I learned later. He repeated the message. Silence. He gave up, turned back down the lights and turned the movie back on. I hid outside and watched the three guys blast out the side entrance and run all the way back to the hotel. The next morning, one of them mentioned this little episode to me and told me he had been so worried he hadn't slept for more than an hour the night before. I told him that the Zone VP was a conservative and a religious man and, that had he caught them, I'm sure he would have fired them by now. So, not to worry. Unless...unless he was going to fire them when he was scheduled to attend the meeting early the next day. Perhaps the best way to address it was to just ask for his forgiveness before he could do anything untoward. On second thought, I told him, that would just be career suicide. If I were him, I would just go back to my hotel room tonight and pray. Somehow, my guidance didn't seem to help him feel more secure. I failed to tell them it had just been my little joke. Never did tell them.

And just one more. I am passing this one along so you know that CEOs can be just as stupid and childlike as...well...anyone.

Desk diving

One of my favorite entertainments while CEO was to spot people passing my office, shout out for them to come in and see me "right now" and then hide under my desk while they tried to figure out where the voice was coming from (and you wonder how I eventually lost that job). I did this dozens of time...never got caught. I could hear them asking for me, "Don...are you here? Mr. Hurzeler...where are you?" They would eventually mumble awhile and then wander off. I would reappear and go back to work, a smile on my face.

One day, a direct report of mine walked by. "Ros...get in here now." Ros virtually hit the brakes and hurried back to my office. I, of course, was already under my desk. Ros was bewildered...and a little worried. She finally tracked down my assistant who was walking back from the copy room. "Mary," she said, "I absolutely heard Don call for me and when I entered his office five seconds later, he was gone. Can you help me find him?" I then heard Mary say, "Did you look under his desk?" No...

looking under my desk had not really occurred to this senior executive who worked for me...me being the CEO/President. I could hear the two of them walking over toward me. Curses! Caught. And I can tell you, there is no easy way to play that one off. Once you are actually caught, age 60 and the CEO, hiding under your desk as you play your little prank...well...it is kind of embarrassing. Embarrassing...but stupid enough to interrupt the stress of the day for a moment.

Remember my saying that much of my humor was designed solely to amuse only me? Well, that same office was often visited by vendors, agents, brokers and industry leaders...all of them wanting something from the business unit that I headed. Many of these folks were my friends. A few were new to me. A couple were assholes. I set a trap for the assholes.

In my office, right behind me on a cabinet was a $200 gold photo frame with an unflattering photo of Linda Tripp in it. You will have to look her up. She was the lady that Monica Lewinsky confided in about her affair with then-President Clinton. She was also the lady who let the world know about that affair. After that revelation, Linda Tripp was "controversial," to say the least.

And so it was a big surprise for anyone who might see that photo prominently displayed behind me. I would watch my visitors look at the photo...look again and then make a decision—just to forget about it or to ask me about it. If they asked me about it, I told them it was an inside joke and then moved the conversation on to some other subject. However, on rare occasions, someone would say, "Why in the world do you have a photo of that fat ugly bitch on your desk?" Bingo...I had just discovered an asshole. I then replied, "In my family we call my sister a patriot." Fun would ensue.

Really hard to imagine how I eventually lost that job.

The Low Life's Club

In about 1980, I was promoted to run an insurance office in Pittsburgh. I had never been to Pittsburgh and knew no one there. I was told I would be in the city for two to three years and then would be brought back into the home office. Two to three years was not much time to build a reputation in a city that was completely new to me. So, I did things...

One of my competitors got access to their company plane and flew their best agents and brokers to the Masters in Augusta each April. Only a few agents got to go on this exclusive trip in the fancy private jet. The rest of the agents and brokers got to watch it on TV, pissed off that they were not there.

I loved those guys (sorry to say that there were only a few gals in that group back then, and happy to say that has changed dramatically over the years). So, I formed the Low Life's Club. The idea was that we would meet for dinner at the worst place in town I could find, go directly from there to what was then called WWF Wrestling at the Civic Arena and adjourn from there to one of the nastiest nude bars I've ever been in, on Liberty Street in downtown Pittsburgh. I think we had about twenty participants for the first Low Life's Club event and dinner was, I swear, at the Greyhound Bus Station.

To say it was a hit would be a major understatement. When it came time to organize the second Low Life's Club event, I had to cut the registration off at fifty agents and brokers. On that occasion I sealed my status in the city. I talked my way into the locker room at the arena and chatted with all the wrestlers...Bruno Sammartino, The Tonga Kid, "Rowdy" Roddy Piper, Mr. Perfect and on and on. Somehow they got the impression that I was the local promoter. I went back to my seat and grabbed my marketing guy, Rich Turocy. Rich was and is a sports fanatic and he was in heaven...Bruno was his hero. I told Rich that I had arranged for us to go into the ring with the wrestlers for the main event...a tag team match starring Rowdy, The Tonga Kid, Jimmy "Superfly" Snuka and Mr. Wonderful aka Paul Orndorff. And so I did. Rich had the good sense to veer off at the last minute.

I stood at the beginning of the tunnel that leads to the ring and held my hands on the chests of The Tonga Kid and "Rowdy" Roddy...telling them to let the music build until I said to go. The music blared. Spotlights lit us up. I gave the word and led them into the ring. A police officer was nice enough to hold the ropes open for me while the wrestlers jumped over and under the ropes to get in the ring. By now, I was bouncing around the ring and waving at my agents and brokers. They seemed surprised to see me in the ring for the main event in front of some 16,000 screaming fans. And then, "Rowdy" Roddy Piper hit Jimmy "Superfly" Snuka over the head with a folding chair, just inches from me. That was my exit call and I took it. I signed a few autographs on the way back to the locker room, picked up Rich and took a few refreshing moments at the sink to clean up and get ready for our main event, the strip club.

Looking back, it is hard for me to understand why I never made it to the top deck of the Allstate Insurance company or their independent agent and broker commercial insurance company, Northbrook P&C. Had it been put up to an agent and broker vote, I would have made it.

By the way, we eventually did a Low Life's Club event that included women and spouses. Oddly enough, I made the difficult decision to leave the strip club stop out for that event. I remember my wife asking if she should wear her mink coat to the wrestling event. I told her to wear something that would protect her from spit. She did not enjoy the wrestling crowd as much as I did.

The event got so big that the general manager of the Pittsburgh Penguins heard about it and wanted in on the action. I checked our sign-up sheet and saw that we now had nearly 200 people wanting to go. In my one moment of good sense, I retired that event and did my best to get transferred out of Pittsburgh and back to home office. I could see this turning into big trouble just around the corner. I made it out of town in time...but, man, I sure had fun in Pittsburgh.

The urinal deodorant

I was the Underwriting Department Manager for Allstate Commercial in Brea, California, reported to the big boss and supervised well over one hundred employees. Two doors down from me was the office of my former boss, the marketing manager...who also reported to the big boss. I am not sure what he did to me, but at one point he pissed me off no end. I do not get mad, I get even. So, I broke into the janitor's closet and stole one of those white deodorant things that are often found at the bottom of a urinal. They give off a distinct smell when they get wet. Perfect.

I took that urinal cookie, as most of the men in the office called them in those days, and sewed it into the lining of his drapes. Sewed it in pretty cleverly, in an area where it would be hard to see but where it would release its distinctive smell directly into the air conditioning stream.

My next move was to buy a squirt gun. I filled that squirt gun and then, every morning that I beat him to work (about ten days out of ten), I would go into his office and soak that urinal cookie. By the time he arrived, his office smelled almost exactly like the men's room.

Everyone you can think of tried to find the source of that smell. The janitor tried. The maintenance guy tried. The air conditioning people checked to see if his office was somehow connected to the men's room. He tried. The big boss tried. No joy...still smelled like the men's room.

Took about a year for that urinal cookie to melt down to nothing. I never told anyone what I had done. Guess I have now.

"He who laughs, lasts." —Mary Pettibone Poole

CHAPTER TWENTY-ONE

And In Conclusion

Well, that is what happened to Don during his first 73 years. Adventure, achievement, responsibilities met, injuries sustained, stupidity engaged in and a bunch of childishly silly behavior accomplished in order to keep me marginally sane.

Along the way, I managed to make it through college, have a forty-year successful business career, do a bunch of serious volunteer and charitable work, stay married for fifty years, raise a couple of terrific kids, hold onto some of the world's greatest friends, honor those around me, author a long-running newspaper column and a number of long-lived blogs, write several books, run my own publishing company, stay off booze and cigarettes for the past several decades, avoid drugs in any form, stay out of jail so far, take great care of my closest relatives when they needed me most, be a good partner in a first-class photo gallery business and learn to use a camera with the best of them.

I am neither rich nor poor, but I can pay all of my own bills. I am a happy camper. I am a very happy camper. I am appreciative to God for giving me this long life and so many challenges. The cancer I faced two decades ago made me realize that none of us will be around forever, so I enjoy each day.

What's left of Don?

Courage...that seems to be gaining strength as I cast off former fears and just plain go for it. I am, in no way, fearless...I can "fear" with best of them. However, I have learned to control that fear and to be courageous enough to push myself well past life-long limits, and I have seen the rewards of that courage.

A grasp of "simple"...understanding now that our friends and experiences are WAY more important than physical possessions (except cameras and surfboards).

Appreciation for each day, my wife and my life.

And EGBOK...an old Los Angeles, California, radio team expression (Everything's Going to Be OK) from the Lohman and Barkley comedy radio show. It is all okay... we come, we go and the world goes on. Happy for the run so far and excited for whatever comes next.

Thanks for the read...hope you enjoyed it.

ABOUT THE AUTHOR

Donald J. Hurzeler, CPCU, CLU was born and raised in Southern California. He and his wife, Linda, have lived all over the United States and retired to Kailua-Kona, Hawaii.

Don has an A.A. degree in insurance, a B.A. degree in business and CPCU and CLU professional designations. He has taken graduate-level courses at Northwestern's Kellogg School of Business and at Harvard University.

Over a forty-year corporate career, Don held jobs that put him in charge of training, communications, marketing and underwriting. He was a department head, branch manager, Chief Sales Officer and Chief Marketing Officer. He served as Chief Underwriting Officer for Zurich U.S. and was also the CEO/President of Zurich Middle Markets, a billion-dollar part of the Zurich Financial Services organization. Don was president of the Zurich Foundation, president of a local United Way, national president of the 20,000-member Chartered Property and Casualty Underwriters Society and a member of the board of directors of American Nuclear Insurers.

Don loves to write and has been a writer all his life. He was a columnist for the Barrington (Illinois) Courier-Review and for various insurance-related publications including Best's Review. His first book, Designated for Success, was published in 2004. His second book, The Way Up: How to Keep Your Career Moving in the Right Direction, won a gold medal in the Career category from Axiom Business Books Awards in 2011. His third book, Smells Like Retirement, was published in 2016. Don learned enough about publishing to open his own publishing company, Kua Bay Publishing LLC, and uses that company to publish both his own books and the books of selected other authors...okay, mostly his own books.

Don is a speechwriter who has written for executives at both Allstate Insurance and Zurich Financial Services. He has done extensive public speaking, including keynote addresses, to business groups and university students in the United States and in Europe...and once, quite memorably, after driving all night through a snowstorm to get there, he spoke in front of just five people in Iowa who had braved the weather to enjoy the free breakfast and speech.

Don was the 2005 Golden Torch Award honoree for leadership and innovation within the insurance community, an honor bestowed by the Insurance Marketing & Communications Association (IMCA).

A 1969 NCAA Division II Track and Field All-American, Don is a member of the Chapman University Athletic Hall of Fame and Palos Verdes High School Track Wall of Fame. He is a "middle of the pack" marathon runner who has run both the Pikes Peak Marathon and a marathon inside a cave in Holland. He is also a life-long surfer and dedicated ocean guy.

Don has been married for fifty years to Linda. They have a son, Jim Hurzeler, and a daughter, Stephanie Stanczak, and five grandchildren, Sam, Zack and Julia Hurzeler and Ava and Nathan Stanczak.

Don retired from corporate life in 2008. He and Linda are now partners with C.J. Kale in their gallery business, Lava Light Galleries, Inc. As a landscape photographer, Don has won a number of awards, including the prestigious 2019 Nature's Best Photography's Windland Smith Rice International Award for the Small World category.

Lava Light Galleries is located in Waikoloa, Hawaii, in the Queens MarketPlace. Their website can be found at www.lavalightgalleries.com

You can contact Don through his writing website, www.donhurzeler.com

ACKNOWLEDGEMENTS

A big thank you to my wife, Linda. The day after I retired in 2008, she and I drove to the East Coast from Chicago. It was a long drive and to pass the time, I barked out one-line reminders of stories from our lives and she wrote them down. I used that list of stories to build a good part of this book. Thank you Linda...and thanks for patiently listening to my first read of it, a very long read before the edit.

Thanks to Bob Gorman, my long time editor and friend. Bob fills me with courage, encouragement and often keeps me from making a complete fool of myself, with the possible exception of this time around. Bob consulted with me on this book.

Thank you to Steve Willoughby who saw a mention of this book being written on a Facebook post. Steve asked if I had included the story about the blind lady in NYC...and I had not. I got back to my computer and added that story and send my thanks to Steve for his reminder.

Big thanks to Steve Bennett of Authorbytes. If you look behind the curtain of Kua Bay Publishing LLC, you will find Steve. Steve is the one who gets it done. He is also a muse for me and helps me to think quite differently about the books I intend to write. Oh, and he and his team put together the best author websites in the business. Thank you, Steve, and thanks to all of Team Authorbytes.

Steve has a team of people who responsible for the pieces of putting together my books and websites. One of those is Dan Snow. Dan has been a big help to me for years and I very much appreciate his assistance and friendship. Another is Ken Wiesner...a real pro and always good to have on your side. Laura Spinella has been a huge help in the design of both my book cover and website...thank you Laura.

A giant THANK YOU goes out to Tanya H. Lee. Tanya did the edit on this book and did it quickly and with a lot of thought. She encouraged me to keep in some of the things that I thought might be too silly or awkward...and talked me out of one section that WAS too silly and too awkward...and I appreciate the good advice in both cases. Thank you, Tanya.

Last, I want to thank C.J. Kale for his cover photo of Linda and me, for his friendship of over a decade now and for being a terrific coach/mentor/safety backup and business partner. Without C.J. this book would have been a pamphlet.

Made in USA - Kendallville, IN
13873_9780998106366
09.17.2022 1300